THE
INSTANT POT
BABY FOOD
COOKBOOK

Inspiring | Educating | Creating | Entertaining

Brimming with creative inspiration, how-to projects, and useful information to enrich your everyday life, Quarto Knows is a favorite destination for those pursuing their interests and passions. Visit our site and dig deeper with our books into your area of interest: Quarto Creates, Quarto Cooks, Quarto Homes, Quarto Lives, Quarto Drives, Quarto Explores, Quarto Gifts, or Quarto Kids.

First Published in 2019 by The Harvard Common Press, an imprint of The Quarto Group, 100 Cummings Center, Suite 265-D, Beverly, MA 01915, USA.
T (978) 282-9590 F (978) 283-2742 QuartoKnows.com

The Harvard Common Press titles are also available at discount for retail, wholesale, promotional, and bulk purchase. For details, contact the Special Sales Manager by email at specialsales@quarto.com or by mail at The Quarto Group, Attn: Special Sales Manager, 100 Cummings Center, Suite 265-D, Beverly, MA 01915, USA.

23 22 21 20 19   1 2 3 4 5

ISBN: 978-1-55832-965-2

Digital edition published in 2019
eISBN: 978-1-55832-966-9

Library of Congress Cataloging-in-Publication Data

Names: Schieving, Barbara, author. | McDaniel, Jennifer, author.
Title: The instant pot baby food cookbook : wholesome recipes that cook up
   fast-in any brand of electric pressure cooker / Barbara Schieving,
   Jennifer Schieving McDaniel.
Description: Beverly, MA, USA : Harvard Common Press, 2019. | Includes index.
Identifiers: LCCN 2018053922 | ISBN 9781558329652 (trade pbk.)
Subjects: LCSH: Baby foods--Nutrition. | Pressure cooking. | Electric
   cooking, Slow. | Infants--Nutrition. | LCGFT: Cookbooks.
Classification: LCC RJ216 .S395 2019 | DDC 641.5/6222--dc23 LC record available at https://lccn.loc.gov/2018053922

Cover Image: Shutterstock.com
Page Layout: Gabi Rosoff
Illustration: Shutterstock.com

Printed in China

The information in this book is for educational purposes only. It is not intended to replace the advice of a physician or medical practitioner. Please see your health-care provider before beginning any new health program.

THE
INSTANT POT
BABY FOOD
COOKBOOK

Wholesome Recipes That Cook Up Fast—in
Any Brand of Electric Pressure Cooker

Barbara Schieving
Jennifer Schieving McDaniel

HARVARD
COMMON
PRESS

CONTENTS

DEDICATION

To all the time-crunched moms and dads doing their best to feed their families nutritious and delicious food and to our families, friends, and readers who share our passion for pressure cooking and out love of good food—this cookbook is dedicated to you. Thanks for your support.

AUTHORS' NOTE

The first year of a baby's life is magical and wondrous. It can also be exhausting and frustrating, as you navigate uncharted territory and strive to do just the right things to give your baby a great start in life.

In this cookbook, we've done our best to help make feeding your baby easier and faster. The pressure cooker is a fantastic tool you can use to create healthy, nutritious meals for your baby.

The food habits you want for your children in elementary school and beyond won't magically develop when they hit a certain age—these habits are built from the very beginning. Give your baby a strong start by using these recipes to introduce them to a wide variety of healthy and delicious fruits, vegetables, grains, and meats.

In addition to the delicious recipes, we've included lots of tips and information gathered from a variety of reliable sources that will help you feel confident that you are doing an awesome job as a parent.

Thanks for being a part of our pressure cooking journey. We hope your baby enjoys these first foods and you enjoy your first meals together.

—*Barbara Schieving*

—*Jennifer Schieving McDaniel*

INTRODUCTION

Whenever possible, we try to cook our family's meals from scratch; not only is the food better tasting, but you know exactly what ingredients you're eating. If you've ever tried commercial baby food, you'll know that this same principle applies to from-scratch baby food—it just tastes better!

While it can seem intimidating to cook baby food from scratch, an electric pressure cooker makes it easy to cook nutritious food fast. We're here to show you that, with very little planning, you can make your baby food with fresh ingredients without having to spend hours in the kitchen.

We've included a wide variety of recipes in this book that will take you through baby's first foods to baby's first birthday celebration. Whether you plan to cook just a few foods, batch cook a week's worth of meals, or make every bit of your baby's food from scratch, this book will guide you through the process.

Our Approach

Believe it or not, research from the American Academy of Pediatrics indicates that your baby's food preferences start to solidify at just nine months old. Therefore, we believe one of the best things you can do when introducing solid foods is expose your baby to a wide variety of healthy and great-tasting fruits, vegetables, grains, and meats.

As with so many other things relating to babies, many people have strong opinions when it comes to food. Nursing vs. formula feeding, organic vs. conventionally grown, baby-led weaning vs. traditional solids—it can feel exhausting, especially to new parents who want to "get it right" for their baby.

Ultimately, we believe that there are many wonderful approaches to pressure cooking and many great approaches to feeding your baby. The "right" form of cooking is the one that works with the time you have and the way you want to feed your family—there is no parent-shaming in this book!

These recipes are shaped by our experiences feeding our babies as well as basics recommended by the American Academy of Pediatrics. We've divided the recipes into sections based on food type to make it easier for you to use. The book starts with recipes for single-ingredient fruits and vegetables and then moves on to grains and legumes, fruit and vegetable blends, and meats and dinners, but how you want to use the recipes is up to you! Whether you plan to make everything for your baby from scratch or not, do what works best for you and your family.

Baby Feeding Basics

Food Introduction Timeline

If you're wondering how to go about introducing solid foods—which food to start with, how much food to give, and how quickly to introduce new foods—you're in good company! Starting solids can feel like a big deal, but it's actually pretty simple. Throughout the process, if you're watching your baby's cues and feeding accordingly, you can feel confident your baby is getting the nutrition they need.

For your convenience, we've outlined a general timeline here based on our pediatricians' recommendations as well as current guidelines given by the American Academy of Pediatrics. Remember that babies' needs can vary widely, so talk with your pediatrician throughout this first year for recommendations tailored specifically to your baby and your family's preferences.

Before Solids. The American Academy of Pediatrics generally recommends exclusively feeding babies breast milk or formula for the first six months of life, though there are instances where your pediatrician will recommend starting solids before the six-month mark.

Regardless of age, babies need to achieve certain physical milestones before they can start solids. General signs babies are ready for first foods include:

- ☑ They can hold their head steady and turn their head side-to-side as desired.

- ☑ They are generally able to sit on their own, with a little support.

- ☑ They seem interested in eating or in watching other people eat.

- ☑ They open their mouth for food.

- ☑ They have lost the tongue-thrust reflex and no longer automatically push things back out of their mouth.

When your baby is showing these signs, they're ready to start!

Baby's First Feeding

For baby's first feeding, you'll want to choose a time when your baby is happy and a little bit hungry—too hungry and they'll be fussing, too full and they may not be interested in eating.

Prepare your baby's first food. While single grains like rice cereal have traditionally been the first-food of choice, it's up to you to decide whether you'd prefer to start with cereals, fruits, or vegetables. We chose to start with rice cereal thinned with expressed breast milk or formula in hopes that a familiar flavor would lead to a good first food experience. However, others swear by starting with yellow and orange vegetables and then moving into green vegetables, then fruits, and then grains.

Regardless of what you choose to start with, the key is to start with about 1 tablespoon (15 ml) of a single ingredient in a smooth, thin puree. Choose a soft baby spoon and a bib—first feedings can get messy!

When your food is ready, securely strap your baby into a high chair or have your partner hold your baby upright on their lap. Scoop a small spoonful of food and place it in front of your baby. Talk to your baby and model opening your mouth.

If your baby doesn't open their mouth when you present the food, dab a little on their lips; they'll likely lick their lips and get a taste. If they're still not interested, dab a little food on their tray and let them interact with the food on their own terms—chances are their messy, food-coated hands will go right to their mouth.

If the food comes right back out but your baby seems interested in food, keep offering bites of food as long as they're interested. However, if your baby appears agitated when the food comes out, don't force the food on them. You want to keep mealtimes positive. Try again in a day or two at a different time of day.

The meal is over as soon as your baby starts acting like they're done—common cues include turning away from the spoon, closing their mouth, or pushing food away. Once you notice these signs, put down the baby spoon and congratulate your baby (and yourself) on a successful first feeding!

First Solids to Eight Months. Remember, at this earliest stage of eating, solid foods are just a bonus—your baby should still be getting most of their nutrition from breast milk or formula. Offer small amounts of new food—as little as 1 teaspoon at first and work up to 1 tablespoon (15 g) twice a day around six months and then up to 8 ounces (225 g) of solids per day by eight months.

Introduce one food at a time and watch for reactions for a few days before introducing another new food. (Mild reactions like gas, diarrhea, or a rash may indicate a food sensitivity. More severe reactions like swelling or vomiting can indicate a food allergy.) Once your baby has eaten one new food for three to five days with no reaction, you can safely leave it in the rotation when you begin introducing another new food. (For example, if you introduce rice cereal and then move on to peaches, you can still serve rice cereal during the waiting period for peaches.)

By the end of this period, your baby should be exposed to a variety of smooth fruits, vegetables, grains, and meats, first served separately and then in combinations.

Eight to Ten Months. At this stage, breast milk or formula will still be your baby's main source of nutrition, but they will start to take in less milk as they increase their solid-food intake and may drop a bottle or breastfeeding session or two during this period. In these months, babies should progress toward having three meals a day with the rest of the family as well as one or two healthy snacks.

At eight months, your baby should be eating fruits, vegetables, grains, and proteins, and you can begin introducing dairy products like plain yogurt and cottage cheese. (We love mixing dairy with fruit purees and diced fruits!) You can also start giving your baby more textured foods like meats mixed with steamed vegetable bits or grains.

Also, once your baby starts trying to grasp things with their finger and thumb, they're ready to start finger foods! Ideal finger foods are soft and easy to swallow and include bite-size cereals like Cheerios, soft fruits like bananas and avocados, toast, scrambled eggs, steamed vegetables, and cooked pasta. As always, make sure pieces are small and safe.

Ten to Twelve Months. Continue expanding your baby's diet by adding new flavors and textures. At this point, you can start adding spices to foods—think cinnamon with applesauce or thyme to chicken noodle soup. (Of course, you'll need to start slowly with the seasonings, and you'll still need to avoid adding extra sugar or salt.) Continue serving thicker foods, which stick more easily to spoons, as well as finely chopped table foods and finger foods.

Around ten months, you'll need to be teaching your baby to feed themselves with a spoon and to drink from a cup. It's guaranteed to be messy at first, but it's a step they need to take on their way to self-feeding.

Twelve to Eighteen Months. By twelve months, a significant portion of your baby's diet should come from solid foods. Keep providing healthy foods from the major food groups prepared different ways and in different combinations. Continue giving your baby mashed food or small bites. At twelve months, you also have the green light to introduce honey, raw berries, citrus fruits, and thin layers of creamy nut butter.

At this stage, make sure your baby's meals include plenty of healthy fats; try avocados, eggs, chia seeds, cheese, fish, low-sugar full-fat yogurt, and, of course, full-fat milk.

Unless counseled otherwise by your pediatrician, around twelve months you can start the switch from formula or breast milk to full-fat cow's milk and from bottles to cups. Many babies do best with a gradual change in milk. With some babies, you might replace an ounce (28 ml) of formula with an ounce (28 ml) of cow's milk for a few days and then increase to 2 ounces (60 ml) of cow's milk. Some babies also prefer their formula warmed, so you can slowly decrease the temperature as you dilute it with cow's milk.

Eighteen to Twenty-Four Months. By twenty-four months, your toddler should be eating the same food as the rest of the family, including healthy fruits, vegetables, proteins, and grains—all in small, toddler-size portions.

You'll notice a big improvement in your child's ability to feed themselves during this period; be sure to provide them with many opportunities. In this stage, most toddlers prefer to feed themselves, so plan meals that can be easily diced into small, toddler-friendly finger foods. Your toddler should also have the ability to drink from a cup and to use a spoon, though they may still be messy until age three or four.

Baby Food Safety

There's so much more to food safety than simply dicing food into small pieces and introducing just one new ingredient at a time. For your convenience, we've highlighted a few food-safety items you should be aware of.

Dish up individual servings. Any food that has touched your baby's spoon should be discarded at the end of the meal, regardless of whether you're using store-bought or homemade baby food. The saliva on the spoon can quickly turn your baby's uneaten food into a bacteria breeding ground. To avoid waste, place only what you think your baby will eat into a baby bowl and feed them from the bowl—you can always add more if they're still hungry.

Follow guidelines for safe food preparation. This includes basics like washing your hands well, keeping raw meats away from other food prep, and sterilizing your countertops and cutting boards. Wash and scrub your fruits and vegetables before chopping.

Once cooked, food must be refrigerated or frozen within 2 hours or discarded, and the sooner you can get leftovers in the fridge, the better. Once food is refrigerated, be sure to use or freeze according to USDA baby food standards, which are stricter than food standards for older kids and adults.

Cooked Baby Food	Refrigerator	Freezer
Pureed fruits and vegetables	1 to 2 days	1 to 2 months
Pureed grains and legumes	2 to 3 days	1 to 2 months
Pureed meats and eggs	1 day	1 to 2 months
Meat/vegetable combinations	1 to 2 days	1 to 2 months

Thaw foods in the refrigerator or in cold water, never on the counter at room temperature. And, of course, use your judgment—when in doubt, throw it out!

Know your nitrates. Nitrates are a naturally occurring compound found in soil and well water. In terms of baby food, higher nitrate levels can be found in root and leafy vegetables like carrots, squash, green beans, broccoli, and especially spinach. The American Academy of Pediatrics determined that babies three months and under are most at risk from nitrates, followed by babies six months and under.

Because nitrates occur in the soil, even organic vegetables and commercially prepared baby foods contain them. If you're concerned about nitrate levels in your baby's food, after pressure cooking vegetables, discard the cooking water and use fresh water to make your purees. (Our recipes generally recommend using the cooking water in the purees in order to retain the vitamins and nutrients that are released into the water during the pressure cooking process.) You can also switch up your food schedule to introduce fruits and grains first and then introduce vegetables when your baby is a little older.

Avoid or limit intake of certain foods. There are a number of foods that are not suitable for babies before age one. These foods are discouraged for a variety of reasons, from contaminants to bacteria to proteins that your baby's digestive system isn't mature enough to handle.

- *Honey*. Pediatricians strongly recommend not giving your baby honey or any food containing honey until after your baby's first birthday. (This includes raw honey, wild honey, commercially prepared honey, and even baked goods containing honey.) Honey is a potential source of the bacteria spores that cause botulism, a dangerous gastrointestinal condition that affects the nervous system. Generally, by age one your baby's intestines will have matured enough that infant botulism is no longer a worry.

- *Rice*. White and brown rice and its derivatives (such as rice milk, rice flour, and brown rice syrup) are a potential source of arsenic for both babies and adults because rice tends to absorb higher amounts of arsenic from the soil and water. However, rather than avoiding rice altogether, the American Academy of Pediatrics recommends simply being aware of this and reducing potential exposure by serving your baby (and family) a wide variety of grains. The FDA also recommends that parents consider options other than rice cereal for first foods.

- *Juice*. In addition to being discouraged for low fiber and high sugar content, surprisingly, fruit juices are discouraged because they're another potential source of arsenic. Avoid giving juice to babies under twelve months unless recommended by pediatrician—for instance, prune juice to relieve constipation. After twelve months, the recommended amount is just 4 ounces (120 ml) per day served in an open cup.

- *Certain fish*. This one is tricky—some fish can be great for babies, with amino acids and omega-3s; however, many fish have high mercury levels and are not suitable for babies or toddlers. Avoid mackerel, roughy, bluefin tuna, and many shellfish and check local advisories before feeding your baby freshly caught fish. Recommended fish include codfish, haddock, salmon, tilapia, and canned light tuna.

- *Cow's milk or soy milk*. Although dairy items like yogurt and cheese are encouraged before age one, cow's milk and soy milk should be avoided until after your baby's first birthday. The fats, proteins, and minerals in cow's milk are difficult for babies to digest before one year, and soy milk does not have the nutrients babies need. (Note that soy milk is different from soy-based infant formulas.) Since too much cow's milk inhibits iron absorption, after twelve months, the American Academy of Pediatrics recommends about 16 ounces (475 ml) of full-fat milk a day with a maximum of 24 ounces (700 ml). Soy milk contains lower amounts of calcium, fat, and protein; talk with your pediatrician before introducing it as a replacement for cow's milk.

Test the temperature before serving. While we recommend serving your baby food at a variety of temperatures, be sure to get in the habit of checking the temperature for any food you warm. Microwaves heat food unevenly and create hot spots in the food, and baby food heated on the stovetop may be warmer on the bottom than on top. To address this, stir the food well after warming, let it stand for 30 seconds to a minute and then test the temperature of the food on your lower lip or wrist.

If you're concerned, you can use an instant-read thermometer to make sure the food is below 99°F (37°C) before serving.

Be alert to choking hazards. Whole foods can be potential choking hazards. Foods larger than ½ inch (1.3 cm)—whole blueberries, grapes, cherry tomatoes, nuts, hot dogs, and blocks of cheese—should be sliced into quarters vertically. Foods that may be stringy, like beef, orange segments, and celery, should be sliced into very narrow sections and fully separated before serving. Nut butters, including peanut butter, should be thinned with a liquid if served as a dip or spread very thinly on bread.

Other foods can present a choking hazard even when diced small, including diced fruits and vegetables like raw apples and carrots, raisins and other dried fruit, and nuts and seeds. Squishy foods like marshmallows, large pieces of bread and rolls, and fruit snacks can also present a choking hazard to babies and toddlers. If you wish to serve these foods, give your child one piece at a time and wait until they swallow before giving them another piece. The American Academy of Pediatrics also recommends children avoid popcorn until age four.

Finally, get in the habit of giving your full attention to your baby during mealtimes. Don't leave your baby unattended while eating, turn off the TV, and avoid scrolling on your phone during meals, just to be safe.

Watch for reactions to certain foods. Food sensitivities affect the digestive system and are different from actual allergies, which involve the immune system. Still, if your baby has a food sensitivity, it can be hard on their little tummies. Here are some foods to watch out for; if you suspect your baby is sensitive to these foods, give them a rest for a month or two and then try them again.

- *Gas-producing foods.* Beans, lentils, and other high-fiber foods like broccoli and cauliflower are a good source of iron and a natural way to fend off constipation. Unfortunately, their high fiber content may also make your baby gassy. Starches, like breads, grains, and potatoes, as well as some fruits and dairy may also have this effect on your baby's sensitive tummy. Start by giving your baby a small amount of these foods and then watch them closely for tummy troubles.

- *Acidic fruits and vegetables.* Foods with a high acid content—think strawberries, oranges, pineapples, and tomatoes—may be hard on some babies or cause a mild skin rash around their lips or in their diapers. Generally, these reactions are more common when these fruits and vegetables are served raw than when they've been cooked and pureed.

- *Foods that cause constipation.* Foods particularly likely to cause constipation include starchy foods like breads, rice, and potatoes, as well as bananas, apples, and dairy. In the beginning, just introducing solid foods can sometimes cause problems for babies' sensitive tummies. Prunes, both pureed and juiced, are your first line of defense (if your baby will take them). You can also introduce more high-fiber foods into your child's diet. If constipation is more than an occasional problem, be sure to talk to your pediatrician.

- *Water.* Water should not be a significant part of your baby's diet; your baby should receive all of the fluids they need from breast milk or formula. Exceptions to this rule are when it's really hot outside, if your baby appears constipated, or once your baby is old enough to practice drinking from a cup.

A Note about Allergies

For many years, pediatricians recommended delaying introduction of potential allergens like peanuts, eggs, and dairy until after age one—and even later in children who have a parent or sibling with an allergy. These recommendations began to change in 2008, when the American Academy of Pediatrics announced that there is no convincing evidence that delaying introduction of solid foods, including common allergens, past four to six months will have "a significant protective effect." Recent research may even indicate that early introduction of these allergens actually *lessens* your baby's risk of developing food allergies later in childhood.

However, because the science isn't settled yet, we recommend following your pediatrician's advice regarding food introduction. If your child displays any serious signs of food allergies, such as hives, face and tongue swelling, or vomiting, stop the new food immediately and contact your pediatrician. For severe allergic reactions, call 911.

Substitute any ingredients in this cookbook that your pediatrician has recommended avoiding due to your child's previous reactions to foods or your family history of allergens.

Mealtime Tips

Keep in mind that we're not doctors or psychologists—just a mother-daughter team that has done our best to get healthy foods in our babies without stressing too much! However, after all these years feeding kids, we do have a few tricks up our sleeves, supported by recent guidelines from pediatricians and parenting experts. (See the Resources section on page 31 for some of our favorites.)

Make mealtimes upbeat, affectionate, and relaxed. Let's face it: mealtimes with babies can feel long and frustrating—especially when your baby makes a huge mess or just flat out rejects the foods you're trying to serve. However, since the main goal of introducing solid foods is to set the foundation for a healthy lifetime relationship with food, do what you can to establish an upbeat, relaxed approach to mealtimes for both you and your baby.

For parents, remember that a big part of keeping mealtimes relaxed is planning meals ahead of time and based around your schedule. Plan to tackle important skills like self-feeding when you're not in a rush and have time to give your baby a full-on bath if needed. If the mess stresses you out, put a splat mat under the high chair or strip your baby down to their diaper. When eating out or with friends and extended family, pull out less-messy finger foods and only give them a little at a time to reduce messes.

For your baby, so much of their experience depends on their personality: some babies are eager to taste anything you put in front of them, while others clamp their mouths shut at the sight of a spoon. Some babies eat quickly, others take their time; some love purees, others prefer finger foods; and some eat quite a bit, others just nibble. No matter what your baby's approach is to eating, help them stay relaxed by following their cues. Don't force your baby to finish food they don't like or eat if they're not hungry. End the meal once their attention has waned.

Foster connection at mealtimes. Family meals are an important time for connection, especially as your children grow beyond the toddler years. Starting with their very first meals, make mealtimes a connection point with your baby.

Turn off the TV, put away your cell phone, and minimize other distractions. Make eye contact and talk to your baby throughout the feeding process. Once your baby begins to vocalize, "chat" back and forth with them about the foods they're eating. Acknowledge when they like or don't like something.

Another way to foster connection is to establish a routine around eating and give your baby clear signals throughout. Whether you use sign language or sing songs, use clear signals to indicate the start and end of mealtimes as well as different points in the meal, like getting in the high chair or putting on the bib. We used simple signs (like *more, all done, milk*), and there's just something adorable about watching your baby enthusiastically sign "more" before each bite. We found that signs helped make our babies active participants in the feeding process and began opening communication even before they could speak.

Offer the same food multiple times. Research from the American Academy of Pediatrics has shown that it can take as many as twenty exposures to a new food before a baby accepts it. If your baby doesn't like a food, don't force them to eat it. However, don't take it off the menu either! Wait a week or two and then try it again —and again and again, as necessary.

Also, try serving the food in different ways—mix it with cereal, yogurt, or cottage cheese; blend it with another food that your baby prefers; or try dicing it small and serving it as a finger food. Keep trying!

Serve meals strategically. Offer new or less-favorite foods first and save favorite foods for later in the meal. Similarly, serve vegetables and lower-sugar foods first and save sweet foods like fruits for the end of the meal.

Also, apply this principle throughout the day: serve new or less-favorite foods when your baby is awake and in a good mood and save favorite, familiar foods for when your baby is tired or more likely to be fussy.

Set up healthy habits. The American Academy of Pediatrics recommends parents serve fruits or veggies at every meal. Exposing your baby to many different fresh flavors and textures and to foods made from fresh produce and home-cooked meats teaches them to eat right and love real foods from the beginning. This is a healthy habit that will serve them well throughout their life. (And it might even encourage you to add more fruits and vegetables to your meals as well.)

Making Baby Food

Here are the basics you need to know to get started making nutritious, delicious foods for your baby.

Cooking Baby Food

The recipes walk you through the process of making the purees. Prepare your ingredients by washing your produce well, rinsing your grains and beans, and trimming your meats. Cook the food according to the recipe. Don't be afraid to experiment with the recipes—if you find adding a minute or two at high pressure helps your foods blend better, go for it! Or, if you want your purees to be a little more textured for older eaters, take a minute or two off the cook time. (It's baby food, not fine French cuisine. Just make sure the meats are cooked through.)

Once the foods are cooked, we like to transfer the cooked foods to a bowl to cool and reserve the cooking water in a glass or a measuring cup with a pour spout. This frees you up to either start another batch of food in the pressure cooker or clean your pressure cooker while the food cools.

When you're ready to puree, make sure you don't overfill your blender or food processor. Add enough liquid that the foods can blend without being too thin. If you want your purees to be smooth like commercial baby food, you'll need to use a high-powered blender. Blend at a low speed for about 10 seconds to break down the ingredients and then blend for another 20 seconds at a high speed for smooth purees. If you don't have a high-powered blender but still want your purees as smooth as possible, just puree the foods as smooth as you can and then pass them through a fine-mesh strainer.

If you're serving the baby food immediately, make sure it's cooled enough to be safe for your baby. Refrigerate the portion you plan to serve in the next day or two and then transfer the remainder of the baby food to freezer-safe containers.

Making multiple foods in one session. When using the steamer basket for purees, start with the easiest recipe to prepare. While the first batch is in the pressure cooker, start preparing the ingredients for the next batch. When your first batch is finished cooking, empty the contents of the steamer basket, rinse out the pot and steamer basket, and start the next batch. (If you're using the steamer basket again, don't forget to add the cup (235 ml) of water in the bottom before locking the lid! It can be easy to forget when you're making many foods in one session.) If you're making any meats, be sure to save those for the end of the pressure cooking session.

Make multiple purees at the same time. You can use pot-in-pot cooking to make more than one puree at a time. For instance, using wide-mouth mason jars, you can make four smaller batches of different purees at the same time. To do this, you need to choose recipes that have similar cook times, such as apples and pears. See 4-in-1-Pot Single-Ingredient Purees (page 56) for an example of this process.

Freezing, Storing, and Thawing Baby Food

Make sure you have selected a container that is freezer-safe, particularly if you're using glass containers to freeze your baby foods. Tightly wrap trays with plastic wrap or secure the lid tightly in place on your freezer-safe containers before freezing.

If you've made several batches of baby food, use masking tape and a permanent marker to label the freezer container. (You may think you'll know which puree is in which container, but many purees can look similar and it gets hard to remember a week later. Make things easy on yourself!)

Once the food is frozen solid, you can transfer the portions to a zipper-top plastic bag. Again, make sure the bag is labeled with the type of food and the date it was cooked. Remove as much air as possible from the bag before sealing tightly.

Store baby food away from the fridge or freezer doors to make sure the food stays as cold as possible. Be sure to use or discard the baby food according to the recommended schedule on page 14.

Sometimes, baby food purees can develop ice crystals on top; this is fine and won't affect the quality of the foods. If you suspect some purees have developed freezer burn, the USDA says that these foods are still safe to eat, just cut away the freezer-burned portions for texture reasons.

Thawing baby food puree. We recommend getting in the habit of planning your baby's meals the night before since the easiest way to thaw your purees is to place them in the fridge overnight. Simply remove the frozen purees you plan to serve, place them in individual bowls, cover, and they'll be ready to serve in the morning. (Do not refreeze foods once they have thawed.) Sometimes, purees defrosted in the refrigerator will have liquids separate out. Give these purees a good stir to reincorporate the liquids.

Some babies are happy to eat foods right out of the refrigerator; however, others prefer their purees to be warmed, at least at first. There are several ways to warm the food—use whichever method aligns with your parenting style.

- *Warm water.* Fill a shallow bowl with hot water. Place the small bowl of baby food puree inside the shallow bowl, checking to make sure the hot water does not come over the top of the baby food bowl. Allow the baby food to sit until it reaches your desired temperature. (This method also works if you forgot to remove the baby food from the freezer the night before; it just takes a little longer to warm through, so you may need to replace the water.)

- *Stovetop.* Place the baby food in a small saucepan. Turn the heat on low and stir the baby food frequently. Add a little liquid if the baby food thickens before it's heated to your desired temperature. Be sure to stir well and test the temperature before serving to your baby.

- *Microwave.* Place the baby food in a glass dish and cook at 50 percent power for 15 seconds. Stir well to avoid hot spots and test the temperature before serving to your baby.

Also, be aware that freezing may change the structure of foods; in some instances, purees that were perfect fresh may take on a different texture when thawed. Some babies won't mind the changes in texture; others may be more sensitive. Here's what you can expect:

- *Fruits and vegetables.* Some fruits and vegetables defrost a little watery, others defrost a little thick. Before deciding to add water, be sure to mix the thawed puree well. For older eaters, you can mix in some diced or mashed fruits to help thicken the puree and change up the texture.

- *Grains and legumes.* We recommend freezing cooked grains and legumes whole in individual, flattened portions. Once frozen solid, transfer frozen portions to a single freezer bag. After defrosting, use a food mill and puree until smooth. (Despite our best efforts, no matter what methods we tried, frozen pureed cereals turned rubbery, watery, and unappealing when defrosted.) Freezing grains and legumes whole also allows you to stir them into purees to add texture for older eaters.

- *Meats and dinners.* Freezing the pureed meats may change the texture and consistency of the puree. Much like the fruits and vegetables, mix the thawed purees well before deciding to add more water. If you wish, you can also freeze the cooked meats in individual portions before pureeing.

Mix and match. When you're thawing baby foods, you don't have to keep everything separate. Thaw a portion of rice with a portion of sweet peas or chicken to make a great meal for your eight-month-old. Combine different flavors of fruit purees with yogurt to make a fun baby breakfast smoothie!

Sterilizing in Your Pressure Cooker

If you wish, you can sterilize or sanitize your bottles and pump parts in your electric pressure cooker. Some models of pressure cookers, like the Instant Pot Duo Plus, have a built-in Sterilize feature, while other brands direct you to use a Steam setting or even the High Pressure setting.

Unfortunately, there is very little official guidance from the major brands on the sterilization process to ensure that your items are sterilized. In addition, there are differences in opinion regarding whether pressure cookers get hot enough or achieve a high enough pressure to truly sanitize (250°F [121°C] at 15 psi), so some people consider this a "sanitizing" feature. Ultimately, not enough testing has been done on sterilizing in the pressure cooker, so we don't recommend it at this time.

However, if you are interested in using the pressure cooker for sanitizing baby bottles or binkies, the common practices are as follows:

- Before sterilizing, make sure your baby bottles, jars, pumps, pacifiers, and utensils are safe for steaming. (Generally, the packaging inserts that come with these items will include information on whether they can be boiled and for how long.)

- Wash these items in warm, soapy water and then rinse well.

- Place 1 cup (235 ml) water in your pressure cooker and use a trivet or steamer basket to elevate the items above the water when steaming. Don't place items directly on the bottom of the pressure cooking pot and don't overfill.

- If your pressure cooker has a Sterilize function, select Sterilize adjusted to high; if not, select Steam or High Pressure and 2 minutes cook time. Use a quick pressure release. (You can increase the cook time or use a natural pressure release if you wish, but be mindful of the items you're steaming; some items may warp at longer cook times.)

Useful Equipment For Making Baby Food

Although we've listed a number of items that will make cooking baby food easier, they're not all mandatory! Try making baby food with what you already have on hand and see what you'd like to add to your collection. Don't feel like you have to run out and buy all of this at once—save that money for diapers!

Blender. Not all blenders are created equal. If you want to make your homemade baby food as smooth as store-bought baby food, you'll need a high-powered blender like Blendtec or Vitamix. These blenders have powerful motors that can handle blending thicker foods with less liquid, and their large blender jars also give you the ability to make large batches of baby food at once.

The baby food recipes in this book were pureed using a high-powered blender to determine the minimum amount of water needed for each recipe. If you are using a traditional blender, you'll likely need to add more water to your baby foods to blend them to a smooth consistency.

Immersion Blender. Immersion blenders, also called "stick blenders," let you blend directly in the pressure cooking pot without having to worry about spilling or waste from transferring to a separate blender jar. Although these appliances are powerful and convenient, they don't blend food quite as smoothly or as uniformly as a high-powered blender and generally require additional water to blend. However, we love them for making thicker, more textured purees for older eaters.

Food Processor. Food processors are also an option for making baby food purees. These machines use a sharp knife to chop and puree foods, and they come in many sizes. Some people prefer using a food processor for making purees because some food processors can use less water and make purees a little thicker; others prefer blenders for their uniform consistency. Try what you have before you decide. We like food processors to make quick work of chopping cheeses and meats for older eaters but prefer blenders for making smooth baby food purees.

Food Mill. Food mills are a great way to puree and strain at the same time. These gadgets come in a wide variety of sizes, from several quarts (6.6 L) on down, and have historically been used for canning. If you plan to make baby foods in big batches and don't mind an arm workout, this will be a wonderful addition to your kitchen. Generally, food mills work well with softer fruits, vegetables, grains, and legumes—many food mills can even filter out the seeds in fruit purees. However, food mills may they can struggle a bit when grinding meats or stringy vegetables like green beans.

For making a single serving of baby food, skip the larger mills in favor of a baby food mill. These smaller mills come in both electric and hand-crank models and allow you to grind up small amounts of food. We particularly love the baby food mills for grinding grains. They won't be as smooth as commercial cereals, but they are perfect for making single-serving meals when baby is ready for some texture.

Masher. Whether you purchase a baby food masher or just use the regular-old potato masher you have around your house, this tool is perfect for older babies who can handle a bit of texture in their soft foods. If you want to get fancy, try a ricer—they're perfect for pressing potatoes and other soft foods into fine purees.

Fine-Mesh Sieve. Also called a "strainer," this kitchen gadget comes in a number of sizes. For baby food, we prefer a small-size strainer because it is less mess to clean up. Although it can be time-consuming, pushing soft fruit and vegetable purees through the sieve with the back of a spoon allows you to remove seeds, skins, or strings.

Kitchen Shears. Although this kitchen gadget isn't necessarily pressure cooker–specific, it is by far our most-used tool for feeding babies finger foods. Whether you call them "shears" or "scissors," these sharp, oversized kitchen scissors make it a snap to snip meats, veggies, and breads into baby-friendly bites either before or after pressure cooking.

Baby Food Freezer Trays. Once you've made the baby food, you'll need something to freeze it in. Although there are a variety of products you can use, from simple ice cube trays to plastic pouches, for younger eaters, we love the baby food freezer trays that allow us to freeze purees in small ¾-ounce (21 g) cubes, which minimizes food waste. For older eaters, we love the round BPA-free silicone baby food trays. Not only are they great for freezing baby food into larger 2-ounce (55 g) servings, but the round trays fit perfectly in a 6-quart (5.7 L) pressure cooker, allowing you to continue to use them after your baby has outgrown purees.

Other Noteworthy Feeding Accessories. Although not necessary for making baby food, there are two other baby accessories worth mentioning. First, find a few good spoons for feeding your baby. For first foods, we love the tiny rubber-coated spoons with a shallow bowl. These spoons make it so easy to scoop a small amount of food, and they protect your baby's gums. However, once baby starts reaching for their own spoon, we prefer shorter, wider spoons with slightly deeper bowls. (The first-foods spoons tend to have longer handles that babies often gag themselves with.) The second accessory we couldn't live without are splat mats. These thick plastic mats go under the high chair and makes for easy cleanup after meals.

✦ Resources

If you're interested in reading in depth about your child's nutrition and development or in learning more about making baby food, we've included some of our favorite books and websites that we've consulted as we've raised our own children. These books represent a range of perspectives on these issues, so some of them may be a better fit for your parenting style than others.

Books

The American Academy of Pediatrics. 2014. *Caring for Your Baby and Young Child, 6th edition*. Edited by Steven P. Shelov and Tanya Remer Altmann.

The American Academy of Pediatrics. 2011. *Nutrition: What Every Parent Needs to Know,* 2nd edition. Edited by William H. Dietz and Loraine Stern.

Nimali Fernando and Melanie Potock. 2015. *Raising a Healthy, Happy Eater: A Parent's Handbook: A Stage-by-Stage Guide to Setting Your Child on the Path to Adventurous Eating.*

Ellyn Satter. 2000. *Child of Mine: Feeding with Love and Good Sense*, revised edition.

William Sears, Martha Sears, Robert Sears, and James Sears. 2013. *The Baby Book: Everything You Need to Know About Your Baby from Birth to Age Two*, revised edition.

Websites

www.healthychildren.org

www.askdrsears.com

www.familydoctor.org

www.foodsafety.gov

www.wholesomebabyfood.com

www.superhealthykids.com

Pressure Cooking Essentials

Using Your Pressure Cooker

The recipes in this cookbook are written to work in all brands of electric pressure cookers, including the Instant Pot. While you may already be familiar with the pressure cooking terminology and settings for your specific device, for your convenience, we've included a brief guide explaining how we've used these terms in this cookbook.

Pressure Cooker Parts

It might look complicated initially, but your electric pressure cooker is actually pretty simple when you get to know it, and all brands have similar components. For questions specific to your particular model, check your user manual.

Housing. This is the outer part of the pressure cooker that contains the buttons and the heating element and is connected to the cord. *DO NOT add ingredients directly to the housing or you may permanently damage your pressure cooker.*

Cooking Pot. This is the inner removable pot, and it's where the magic happens. While you're adding the ingredients to this pot, treat the cooking pot like you treat any pot on the stove—for example, lifting it up off the heating element to slow the cooking. Once you lock the lid in place, however, you'll be unable to access this pot until the pressure is released.

Sealing Ring. This large flexible ring attaches to the underside of the lid. When the lid is locked, the sealing ring prevents steam from escaping, allowing the machine to build pressure inside the pot.

Float Valve and Mini Gasket. This small valve fits inside the lid and is paired with a miniature silicone gasket. When your machine reaches pressure, steam pushes the float valve up and seals the pressure cooker, locking the lid until the float valve drops again, indicating pressure inside the cooker has been released.

Pressure Release Switch. This piece is located on the lid and controls how the pressure inside the pot can escape. In one position, it will seal the steam inside your electric pressure cooker, and in another, it will allow the steam to release quickly. (Depending on your model of electric pressure cooker, this may be called a *switch, valve,* or *button,* but the function is identical.)

Cook Settings

While each model of pressure cooker has different buttons and different functions, most of them are just preset cook times for different foods. *Remember, your pressure cooker CANNOT actually sense what you are cooking and CANNOT tell you when the food in your pot is cooked through.*

Since the recipes in this cookbook were developed for all brands of electric pressure cookers, we avoid the preset button and only use the following settings:

High Pressure/Manual/Pressure Cook. This setting tells the machine to cook at high pressure. When a recipe says, "Select High Pressure and 5 minutes cook time," this will be the setting you use. (The exact name of this setting will depend on the model of electric pressure cooker you own. If your model of pressure cooker doesn't have a manual setting, consult your user guide and choose the preset button with the closest time to the time in the recipe.)

Sauté/Simmer/Browning. This setting allows you to use the cooking pot like any other stovetop pot. Use this setting with the lid off. (Depending on your brand of electric pressure cooker, you may have separate buttons for each heat level or a single button that can adjust the heat level up or down as desired. Some brands don't have a Sauté button, and users select a preset button with the lid off.)

Keep Warm. When the cook time ends, many electric pressure cookers will automatically switch to the Keep Warm setting. Be aware that the contents of your pot will continue to cook as long as this setting is on. This setting can be useful; however, we recommend turning this setting off or unplugging the pressure cooker if you're prone to forgetting to remove the cooking pot from the housing once the meal is complete. And, of course, be sure to turn off your pressure cooker when you're done using it.

Pressure Release Methods

After the cook time has ended, the timer will sound. At this point, the recipe will direct you to release the pressure using the following methods:

Quick Pressure Release. When the cook time ends, turn the pressure release switch to Venting and watch the pressure cooker release a jet of steam. Be sure to position your pressure cooker so that the steam vents away from your cabinets and avoid placing your face or hands directly over the vent, as the steam can burn. If liquid or foam start coming out of the vent, return the switch to the Sealed position for a minute or two and then try venting the pressure again. Wait until the pressure is completely released, the float valve drops, and the lid un-locks easily before trying to open the lid.

Natural Pressure Release. When the cook time ends, just leave the pressure release switch in the Sealed position. The pressure will release slowly through the switch, with no visible jet of steam or noise. With this method, the only way you'll know the pressure is fully released is the float valve will drop and the lid will unlock easily. (It's a bit anticlimactic in comparison.)

Many recipes combine these release methods, instructing you to allow the pressure to release naturally for a certain amount of time and then finish with a quick pressure release. To do this, simply wait the specified number of minutes and then turn the switch from Sealed to Venting to release any remaining pressure.

Pressure Cooking Accessories

A few simple accessories will make cooking a little easier and will help you get even more time savings from your pressure cooker. Some of these items come with your pressure cooker, and you may already own other accessories that can be used in your pressure cooker. Generally, as long as it's an oven-safe dish that fits on a trivet inside the inner cooking pot with room for steam to rise around the dish, it's good to go.

The following accessories are ones we've used in this cookbook; however, you don't need all of these at once. If you're thinking of purchasing some accessories, we recommend starting with an instant-read thermometer, for food safety, and a round cake pan and trivet, since many of our recipes use the pot-in-pot cooking method. Add the other accessories as your budget allows.

Extra Silicone Ring. Because the silicone ring sometimes takes on the smell of your most recent meal, we prefer to have at least two silicone rings for our pressure cooker: one for savory, spicy, or strong-smelling foods and another for breakfasts, fruits, and desserts.

Instant-read Thermometer. Whether it's a fork-style or pen-style thermometer, this important food-safety tool helps you ensure that foods have reached a safe internal temperature. Since cuts of meat can vary widely in size and thickness, it is always wise to check meats for doneness. Common safe internal temperatures are as follows:

Breads and cakes	210 °F (99°C)
Chicken thighs and wings	180 °F (82°C)
Beef (well-done)	165 °F (74°C)
Chicken breasts	165 °F (74°C)
Turkey	165 °F (74°C)
Ground beef	160 °F (71°C)
Pork	145 °F (63°C)

Mason Jars. Wide-mouth mason jars are the perfect size to fit an immersion blender. You can fit up to four tall pint-size (473 ml) wide-mouth mason jars in a 6-quart (5.7 L) pressure cooker, allowing you to cook multiple foods at the same time. (Be aware that common brands make two shapes of pint-size (473 ml) wide-mouth mason jars—short and tall—and only the tall ones fit four at once.)

Retriever Tongs. Many people prefer to use these little grabbers to remove the inner pan from the pressure cooking pot when doing pot-in-pot cooking.

Round Cake Pan. A 7 x 3-inch (18 x 7.5 cm) round cake pan is a pressure cooking must! It's the secret for pot-in-pot cooking, which allows you to cook side dishes and sauces at the same time you cook your meal. If you wish to make the smash cakes in chapter 5, you'll need a 4 x 2-inch (10 x 5 cm) round cake pan.

Silicone Mini-Mitts. These inexpensive, flexible mitts work like hot pads but give you more grip and control when handling a hot pressure cooking pot—and the all-silicone design is easy to clean.

Sling. A sling makes it much easier to remove hot pans from the cooking pot when doing pot-in-pot cooking. You can make your own sling out of a long strip of aluminum foil folded into thirds so it's about 26 inches (66 cm) long by 4 inches (10 cm) wide.

Steamer Basket. A steamer basket keeps foods out of the water and has small holes like a colander. This tool is really useful for cooking foods that break down easily in water and makes them easy to remove from the pressure cooking pot.

Trivet. A trivet (sometimes called a *rack*) keeps ingredients and pots off of the bottom of the pressure cooking pot. Since they are relatively inexpensive, we prefer to have two: a short trivet (½ inch [1.3 cm] or less) for taller items like mason jars and a tall trivet (2 to 3 inches [5 to 7.5 cm] high) for cooking side dishes and sauces over a main dish.

Tips, Tricks, and Troubleshooting

Life with babies is busy enough—the last thing you need is to spend time running to the store in the middle of cooking or fixing a meal that didn't work out. Here are a few tips and tricks that will help you get started.

Know your model size. The recipes in this cookbook were created in and tested using a 6-quart (5.7 L) electric pressure cooker. While these recipes will work in larger pressure cookers, your cook time may be slightly different, and you may need to use more liquid than the recipe calls for. Many of the recipes will also work in smaller pressure cookers; however, the pot-in-pot recipes may need to be cooked separately.

Read the whole recipe before you start cooking. This is a simple thing that has a huge effect on your cooking (and your stress level while cooking)! Reading though the recipe ensures you're familiar with the timing and ingredients, accounts for any resting time, and helps reduce errors. Also, many recipes have serving suggestions at the end, so reading ahead helps you plan when you need to start these items so they'll be ready when you need them.

Prepare your ingredients before cooking. It's frustrating to get halfway through a recipe and realize you're missing a key ingredient. By having your ingredients measured and chopped before you start cooking, you'll be ready for quick transitions and the actual cooking process will go more smoothly.

Trust your senses. Listen to your intuition and don't doubt what you see and smell! For example, if the cook time is up, but your butternut squash doesn't seem quite done, then return the lid and add a few more minutes at High Pressure. Variations in ingredient size and thickness can make a difference in the cook time.

Check the temperature of your meat. Due to variations in size and thickness, the meat in your pot will sometimes need a little longer cook time than the recipe suggests. As soon as you've released the pressure, check the meat for doneness, consulting the temperature guidelines on page 36.

Get familiar with pot-in-pot cooking. When you're cooking pot-in-pot, some foods may take a little longer to cook because they're a little farther from the heating element. (For example, we've found white rice does better with 4 minutes pot-in-pot, compared to 3 minutes when cooked the traditional way.) If something you've cooked pot-in-pot isn't done to your liking, make a note to add another minute or two the next time you make it. Also, if you're steaming something pot-in-pot, try to get in the habit of adding the water to the pot *before* you put the trivet or steamer basket in the cooking pot—just to make sure you don't forget it!

Cook a double batch of favorite recipes. Many of these recipes are easily doubled in a standard 6-quart (5.7 L) pressure cooker without increasing the cook time. However, be aware that if you're doubling, you'll need to make note of the maximum fill line and you may need to extend the natural pressure release if your ingredients are likely to froth or foam.

Solutions to Common Concerns

Once in a while, something goes wrong as you're cooking—it even happens to cooks who aren't distracted by babies! For brand-specific troubleshooting tips, consult your pressure cooker user manual; however, for your convenience, we've included our solutions to the most common concerns we hear about from blog readers, family, and friends.

Steam is coming from my pressure cooker. First, determine where the steam is coming from. If it's coming from the pressure release switch or the float valve, double-check that the pressure release switch is fully in place and turned to the Sealed position. If it's coming from the float valve, use a quick pressure release and remove the lid and then check that the float valve is properly installed and that the mini gasket is tightly in place. If steam is escaping from the sides of the lid, use a quick pressure release and check that the silicone sealing ring is tightly in place around the entire lid. In rare cases, the sealing ring is cracked or broken; in these instances, unfortunately, the only solution is to replace it.

If you notice the steam escaping early in the cooking process, you can simply restart the High Pressure cook time. However, if a number of minutes went by before you noticed the problem, you may need to add more liquid to the cooking pot and reduce the cook time—there's no hard rule for how much, just make your best guess.

My pressure cooker sprays liquid when releasing the steam. This can happen, especially when you're cooking starchy foods like grains, dried beans, or pasta. If water starts to spray during your quick pressure release, return the pressure release switch to the Sealed position. Wait 30 seconds and then open the pressure release switch again and allow pressure to release. If more liquid comes out, repeat the process. With some foods, one or two closed intervals is all you need before you can leave the switch in the Venting position; with other foods, it takes several closed intervals to fully release the pressure.

My food isn't cooked through. If your food is nearly done, select Sauté and finish cooking the dish on that setting for a few minutes. However, if your meat isn't close to the proper temperature or isn't as fall-apart tender as you'd like, lock the lid in place, cook for a few additional minutes at High Pressure and then use the pressure release method called for in the recipe. If quicker-cooking foodslike vegetables or rice are done but your meat is not, remove the quicker-cooking Ingredients from the cooking pot and cover them with aluminum foil before returning the meat to High Pressure.

If "baking" smash cakes in the pressure cooker, make sure you've followed the instructions on whether to bake covered or uncovered because covering the pan with foil has a big effect on the total cook time.

My food stuck to the pan. Make sure that you added enough liquid to the pressure cooking pot and that it was evenly distributed on the bottom of the cooking pot. If cooking pot-in-pot, double-check that you added water to the pressure cooking pot and any required liquids to the pot the food is in. Finally, re-member that larger 8- or 10-quart (7.6 to 9.5 L) pressure cookers may need more liquid than their smaller 6-quart (5.7 L) counterparts.

My silicone ring still smells like yesterday's dinner. Unfortunately, the food-grade silicone that allows pressure cookers to come to pressure also has a tendency to take on the smells of the foods being cooked—we haven't yet come across a brand of pressure cooker that doesn't have this problem. For the most part, the odor will not impact the food you're cooking.

Although there are dozens of methods to remove food smells from the silicone ring—soaking or steaming in lemon juice, vinegar, coffee grounds, tomato juice, and even bleach—we haven't found one that completely gets rid of the smell. To minimize the smell, we prefer to store the silicone rings so they have a chance to air out and to have one ring for savory meats and another for mild fruit purees and desserts.

CHAPTER 1

FIRST FRUITS AND VEGETABLES

When introducing babies to solid foods, pediatricians recommend starting with just one new food at a time. These single-ingredient fruits and vegetables are gentle and great for baby's first solids. Plus, these made-fresh purees look and taste so much better than commercial first foods—you may find yourself eating some of them along with your baby.

APPLE PUREE

Apples are naturally sweet and are loaded with vitamins and fiber. They would make a delicious choice for introducing your baby to fruits. Makes 3½ cups (820 ml).

INGREDIENTS

5 large soft apples (such as Jonagold, Fuji, or Golden Delicious), peeled, cored, and quartered

¼ cup (60 ml) water

METHOD

1. Place the apple quarters and ¼ cup (60 ml) water in the pressure cooking pot. Lock the lid in place. Select High Pressure and 4 minutes cook time.

2. When the cook time ends, turn off the pressure cooker. Let the pressure release naturally for 5 minutes, then finish with a quick pressure release. When the float valve drops, carefully remove the lid. Allow to cool for 20 minutes.

3. Transfer the contents of the cooking pot to a blender jar or food processer and blend until very smooth. (Add water if needed to blend but use the minimum amount necessary.)

TIP

This recipe calls for peeled apples since apple skins have extra fiber, which can affect babies' sensitive tummies. Once your baby is a little older and ready for more texture in foods, you can skip peeling the apples if you prefer.

DRIED APRICOT PUREE

If your baby isn't a fan of prunes, dried apricots have a similar effect with a very different, sweet-tart taste. By using dried, you never have to worry about whether your apricots will be ripe or sweet enough. Makes 1 ½ to 2 cups (355 to 475 ml).

INGREDIENTS

1 cup (130 g) dried apricots, approximately 25   1¾ cups (410 ml) water

METHOD

1. In the pressure cooking pot, add the dried apricots and 1¾ cups (410 ml) water. Stir to ensure the dried apricots are completely submerged. Lock the lid in place. Select High Pressure and 10 minutes cook time.

2. When the cook time ends, turn off the pressure cooker. Let the pressure release naturally for 10 minutes, then finish with a quick pressure release. When the float valve drops, carefully remove the lid.

3. Use a slotted spoon to remove the dried apricots from the pressure cooking pot, reserving the cooking water. Allow to cool for 20 minutes.

4. Place the cooked apricots in a blender jar or food processer and add 1 cup (235 ml) reserved cooking water. Blend until very smooth. (Add more water if needed to blend but use the minimum amount necessary.)

TIP
Check the packaging label and avoid buying dried apricots with sulfates, added sugars, artificial colors, or preservatives.

DRIED PLUM (PRUNE) PUREE

Whether the label calls them "dried plums" or "prunes," these little fruits are the go-to food for keeping baby regular. Makes 1½ to 2 cups (355 to 475 ml).

INGREDIENTS

1 cup (175 g) dried plums, approximately 25

1¾ cups (410 ml) water

METHOD

1. In the pressure cooking pot, add the dried plums and 1¾ cups (410 ml) water. Stir to ensure the plums are completely submerged. Lock the lid in place. Select High Pressure and 10 minutes cook time.

2. When the cook time ends, turn off the pressure cooker. Let the pressure release naturally for 10 minutes, then finish with a quick pressure release. When the float valve drops, carefully remove the lid.

3. Use a slotted spoon to remove the dried plums from the pressure cooking pot, reserving the cooking water. Allow to cool for 20 minutes.

4. Place the cooked plums in a blender jar or food processer and add 1 cup (235 ml) reserved cooking water. Blend until very smooth. (Add more water if needed to blend but use the minimum amount necessary.)

TIP

If your baby isn't a fan of prune puree, try mixing it with other fruit purees, such as apple. If your baby still won't take it, try the Dried Apricot Puree.

NECTARINE PUREE

We prefer nectarines to peaches just because we don't have to bother with the skins. With this recipe, you can blend the puree with the skins on. Makes 3 to 4 cups (700 to 946 ml).

INGREDIENTS

8 large nectarines, halved and pitted

1 cup (235 ml) water

METHOD

1. Place a steamer basket in the bottom of the pressure cooker and add 1 cup (235 ml) water. Then, place the nectarines inside and lock the lid in place. Select High Pressure and 5 minutes cook time.

2. When the cook time ends, turn off the pressure cooker. Let the pressure release naturally for 10 minutes, then finish with a quick pressure release. When the float valve drops, carefully remove the lid.

3. Remove the nectarines from the cooking pot, reserving the cooking water. Allow to cool until comfortable to handle.

4. Place the steamed nectarines in a blender jar or food processer with 1 cup (235 ml) reserved cooking water. Blend until very smooth. (Very juicy nectarines will require less liquid. Add reserved cooking water if needed to blend but use the minimum amount necessary.)

TIP

When selecting nectarines, pick fruit that has a slight give. Nectarines are very easy to halve when they're ripe, but you may still need to use a knife to cut around the pit to remove it. If your nectarines aren't quite ripe enough, place them in a paper bag for a day or two to ripen.

PEACH PUREE

You can use white or yellow peaches with this recipe—white peaches are a little sweeter and less tart, while yellow peaches will result in a traditional golden puree. Makes 3 to 4 cups (700 to 946 ml).

INGREDIENTS

8 large peaches, halved and pitted

1 cup (235 ml) water

METHOD

1. Add 1 cup (235 ml) water to the pressure cooking pot. Add a steamer basket to the pot and place the peaches inside. Lock the lid in place. Select High Pressure and 5 minutes cook time.

2. When the cook time ends, turn off the pressure cooker. Let the pressure release naturally for 10 minutes, then finish with a quick pressure release. When the float valve drops, carefully remove the lid.

3. Remove the peaches from the cooking pot, reserving the cooking water. Allow to cool until comfortable to handle and then peel off the skins.

4. Place the steamed peaches in a blender jar or food processor and blend until very smooth. (Add reserved cooking water if needed to blend but use the minimum amount necessary. Very juicy peaches won't require any additional liquid; less ripe peaches may need up to ½ cup (120 ml).

TIP

If you're using frozen peaches, use a 0-minute cook time and a quick pressure release. If your pressure cooker doesn't allow you to set your cook time for 0 minutes, set your pressure cooker for the minimum time possible and release the pressure as soon as the machine reaches pressure.

PEAR PUREE

Pears are a terrific first fruit for baby. Bartlett pears are a good choice for pear puree because they are soft, mild, and sweet, but you can use this recipe with any variety of pear. Makes 3 to 4 cups (700 to 946 ml).

INGREDIENTS

5 large pears, peeled, cored, and quartered   ½ cup (120 ml) water

METHOD

1. Place the pear quarters and ½ cup (120 ml) water in the pressure cooking pot. Lock the lid in place. Select High Pressure and 4 minutes cook time.

2. When the cook time ends, turn off the pressure cooker. Let the pressure release naturally for 5 minutes, then finish with a quick pressure release. When the float valve drops, carefully remove the lid. Allow to cool for 20 minutes.

3. Transfer the contents of the cooking pot to a blender jar or food processer and blend until very smooth. (Add water if needed to blend but use the minimum amount necessary.)

TIP

If your pears aren't sweet, you can substitute apple juice for the water. If your pears are very ripe, you may not need to cook them as long (or at all)—just puree them in a blender and serve.

BUTTERNUT SQUASH PUREE

There's no need to remove the rind before you pressure cook! After pressure cooking, the softened rind is easy to cut away. Makes 5 to 6 cups 91.2 to 1.4 L).

INGREDIENTS

1 fresh butternut squash

1 cup (235 ml) water

METHOD

1. Wash the butternut squash. Do not peel. Use a sharp knife to remove the ends, cut the neck away from the body, and slice the neck into quarters. Cut the body in half and use a spoon to scrape out the seeds and stringy flesh. Cut each half of the body into quarters.

2. Add 1 cup (235 ml) water to the pressure cooking pot. Add a trivet to the pot and carefully stack the butternut squash pieces on top. Lock the lid in place. Select High Pressure and 5 minutes cook time.

3. When the cook time ends, turn off the pressure cooker. Let the pressure release naturally for 10 minutes, then finish with a quick pressure release. When the float valve drops, carefully remove the lid.

4. Remove the butternut squash from the cooking pot, reserving the cooking water. Allow to cool until comfortable to handle.

5. Use a knife to remove the rind from the butternut squash pieces and place the flesh in a blender jar or food processer. Add ½ cup (120 ml) reserved cooking water and blend until very smooth. (Add more water if needed to blend but use the minimum amount necessary.)

TIP

If you want to skip removing the rind, many grocery and warehouse stores sell prepackaged fresh or frozen cubed butternut squash. Some stores sell the butternut squash in large 2-inch (5 cm) pieces; others come in much smaller ½-inch (1.3 cm) pieces. Place a steamer basket in the bottom of the pressure cooker and place 2 cups (280 g) frozen butternut squash chunks on top. The cook time will depend on the size—for larger pieces, cook for 4 minutes; for smaller pieces, cook for 2 to 3 minutes. This yields about 1½ cups (210 g) squash.

CARROT PUREE

Carrots are easy to digest and packed with fiber and antioxidants like vitamin A. Steaming carrots makes the nutrients even easier to digest, and their sweet flavor often makes them a hit with new eaters. Makes 2 to 3 cups (475 to 700 ml).

INGREDIENTS

8 fresh carrots, peeled and cut into approximately 2-inch (5 cm) pieces

1 cup (235 ml) water

METHOD

1. Place a steamer basket in the bottom of the pressure cooker and add 1 cup (235 ml) water. Place the carrots inside the basket. Lock the lid in place. Select High Pressure and 4 minutes cook time.

2. When the cook time ends, turn off the pressure cooker. Let the pressure release naturally for 10 minutes, then finish with a quick pressure release. When the float valve drops, carefully remove the lid.

3. Remove the carrots from the steamer basket, reserving the cooking water. Allow to cool for 20 minutes.

4. Place the steamed carrots in a blender jar or food processer. Add ¾ cup (175 ml) reserved cooking water and blend until very smooth. (Add more water if needed to blend but use the minimum amount necessary.)

TIP

If you're in a hurry, you can use prepackaged peeled carrots, baby carrots, or frozen carrots. If you're using frozen carrots, use 2 cups (260 g) frozen carrots, a 3-minute cook time, and a quick pressure release.

GREEN BEAN PUREE

Rich in vitamin A and fiber, green beans are a nutritious addition to a baby's diet. Makes 1½ cups (355 ml).

INGREDIENTS

4 cups (400 g) fresh green beans, ends trimmed

1 cup (235 ml) water

METHOD

1. Place a steamer basket in the bottom of the pressure cooker and add 1 cup (235 ml) water. Place the green beans inside the basket. Lock the lid in place. Select High Pressure and 4 minutes cook time.

2. When the cook time ends, turn off the pressure cooker. Let the pressure release naturally for 10 minutes, then finish with a quick pressure release. When the float valve drops, carefully remove the lid.

3. Remove the green beans from the steamer basket, reserving the cooking water. Allow to cool for 20 minutes.

4. Place the steamed green beans in a blender jar or food processer. Add ½ cup (120 ml) reserved cooking water and blend until very smooth. (Add more water if needed to blend but use the minimum amount necessary.)

TIP
Frozen fruits and vegetables are often picked at the peak of freshness, so they are a great option for making baby foods. We often prefer using frozen green beans to skip washing and trimming. If you're using frozen green beans, use 3 cups (372 g) frozen green beans, a 3-minute cook time, and a quick pressure release.

PEA PUREE

Peas make a wonderful first green vegetable for baby—they're on the sweeter side, a good source of fiber, and have a bright green color. Because frozen peas are already shelled and taste great year-round, we generally cook them from frozen; however, you can make purees with fresh shelled peas with no change to the cook time. Makes 1½ cups (355 ml).

INGREDIENTS

2 cups shelled peas (300 g), fresh or (260 g) frozen

1 cup (235 ml) water

METHOD

1. Place a steamer basket in the bottom of the pressure cooker and add 1 cup (235 ml) water. Place the peas inside the basket. Lock the lid in place. Select High Pressure and 2 minutes cook time.

2. When the cook time ends, turn off the pressure cooker. Use a quick pressure release. When the float valve drops, carefully remove the lid.

3. Remove the peas from the steamer basket, reserving the cooking water. Allow to cool for 20 minutes.

4. Place the steamed peas in a blender jar or food processor. Add ¾ cup (175 ml) reserved cooking water and blend until very smooth. (Add more water if needed to blend but use the minimum amount necessary.)

TIP
Sometimes, the outer "skin" of the peas won't puree smooth; if you wish to remove them from the puree before serving, pass them through a fine-mesh sieve.

SPAGHETTI SQUASH PUREE

This squash is easy to cook in the pressure cooker. It has a mild flavor and a beautiful golden color when pureed. Makes about 4 cups (946 ml).

INGREDIENTS

1 fresh spaghetti squash
(about 2 pounds, or 900 g)

1 cup (235 ml) water

METHOD

1. Wash the spaghetti squash. Do not peel. Use a sharp knife to remove the stem end of the squash, cut the squash in half vertically, and remove the seeds with a spoon.

2. Add 1 cup (235 ml) water to the pressure cooking pot. Add a trivet to the pot and carefully place the spaghetti squash pieces on top. Lock the lid in place. Select High Pressure and 8 minutes cook time.

3. When the cook time ends, turn off the pressure cooker. Let the pressure release naturally for 2 minutes, then finish with a quick pressure release. When the float valve drops, carefully remove the lid.

4. Remove the spaghetti squash from the cooking pot, reserving the cooking water. Allow to cool until comfortable to handle and then remove the skin.

5. Place the flesh in a blender jar or food processer. Add ¾ cup (175 ml) reserved cooking water and blend until very smooth. (Add more water if needed to blend but use the minimum amount necessary.)

TIP

When baby is a bit bigger, rather than making a puree, serve this squash as a replacement spaghetti. Cool until comfortable to handle and then use a fork to scrape the strands of "spaghetti" from the skin. We like to serve this when the adults are eating spaghetti—mix the spaghetti squash, some spaghetti pieces, and a little sauce.

SWEET POTATO PUREE

Here are two ways for your baby to enjoy nutritious sweet potatoes: one for when they are just getting started with solid foods, and one for when they are ready for a sweet but healthy treat. Makes 3 to 4 cups (700 to 946 ml).

INGREDIENTS

2 large sweet potatoes

1 cup (235 ml) water

METHOD

1. Peel the sweet potatoes. Cut in half lengthwise and cut into ¼-inch (6 mm) slices. Put a trivet in the bottom of the pressure cooking pot and add 1 cup (235 ml) water. Place the sweet potato slices inside the basket. Lock the lid in place. Select High Pressure and 15 minutes cook time.

2. When the cook time ends, turn off the pressure cooker. Let the pressure release naturally for 10 minutes, then finish with a quick pressure release. When the float valve drops, carefully remove the lid.

3. Remove the sweet potatoes from the pressure cooking pot, reserving the cooking water. Allow to cool for 20 minutes.

4. Place the cooled sweet potatoes in a blender jar or food processer and add ½ to ¾ cup (120 to 175 ml) reserved cooking water. Blend until very smooth. (Add more water if needed to blend but use the minimum amount necessary to get to your preferred consistency.)

Dessert Variation

1 tablespoon (15 g) brown sugar

1 tablespoon (14 g) unsalted butter, melted

¼ teaspoon vanilla extract

¼ teaspoon cinnamon

1 tablespoon (15 ml) heavy cream

Pressure cook the sweet potatoes as directed. When ready to blend, add ½ cup (120 ml) reserved cooking water and the brown sugar, butter, vanilla, and cinnamon and blend until smooth. Add the heavy cream and mix well.

TIP

For this recipe, you'll want to buy the soft sweet potatoes, which have copper skin and orange flesh.

4-IN-1-POT SINGLE-INGREDIENT PUREES

This easy recipe shows you how to make four different purees at the same time—and you can even blend them in the same jars they cook in! Makes four 1-cup (235 ml) servings.

INGREDIENTS

1 to 2 fresh peaches

1 to 2 fresh apples

1 to 2 fresh pears

1½ cups (210 g) frozen diced butternut squash

1 cup (235 ml) water

METHOD

1. Add each ingredient to one of four separate wide-mouth pint-size (473 ml) mason jars. Use as much as will fit in the jar, but do not overfill. Do not place lids on the mason jars.

2. Add 1 cup (235 ml) water to the pressure cooking pot. Add a trivet to the pot and place the mason jars on top. Lock the lid in place. Select High Pressure and 6 minutes cook time.

3. When the cook time ends, turn off the pressure cooker. Let the pressure release naturally for 5 minutes, then finish with a quick pressure release. When the float valve drops, carefully remove the lid.

4. Remove the mason jars from the pressure cooking pot. Allow to cool for 20 minutes and then use an immersion blender directly in the mason jars to puree to your desired consistency.

TIP

This process can be adapted for many different foods. You need to choose recipes that have similar cook times and cooking needs. For example, most frozen fruits and vegetables cook with steam, have similar cook times, and use a short pressure release, so they would work well. Foods like dried prunes that need to cook directly in water would not be a good fit for this process. Because the mason jars shield ingredients from the heat, you may need to increase the cook time by 25 to 50 percent of what was listed in the original recipe.

CHAPTER 2

GRAINS AND LEGUMES

Grains and legumes you make at home are generally not as smooth as commercial cereals, so take that into consideration as you decide when your baby is ready for grains. We've listed the recipes in the order we prefer to introduce them—oats, corn, rice, wheat, quinoa, then legumes; however, use the order that works best for your baby. Since babies eat very small amounts at first, one small batch of grains will last a long time. We like to make a batch and refrigerate enough for a day or two and then freeze the rest in individual portions to combine with fruit or meat purees.

ROLLED OATS

Rolled oats are a wonderful first grain! Once baby is ready for grains, we love to mix these oats with an apple puree. When they're ready for spices, add a little ground cinnamon and this cereal is sure to be a favorite. Makes 1½ cups (351 g).

INGREDIENTS

½ cup (40 g) old-fashioned rolled oats

2 cups (475 ml) water, divided

METHOD

1. Put a trivet in the bottom of the pressure cooking pot and add 1 cup (235 ml) water.

2. In a 7-inch (18 cm) cake pan, stir together the oats and 1 cup (235 ml) water. Use a sling to carefully lower the pan onto the trivet. Lock the lid in place. Select High Pressure and 2 minutes cook time.

3. When the cook time ends, turn off the pressure cooker. Let the pressure release naturally for 5 minutes, then finish with a quick pressure release. When the float valve drops, carefully remove the lid. Use the sling to remove the pan from the pressure cooking pot and allow to cool for 20 minutes.

4. Transfer the cooled oats to a bowl. For younger eaters, use a baby food mill to puree until smooth.

TIP

Be sure to avoid using instant or quick oats in this recipe. Instant and quick oats are rolled thinner and chopped more finely, so they cook too quickly for the pressure cooker.

STEEL CUT OATS

Steel cut oats are the least processed form of oats with the lowest glycemic index. They also cook up a bit chunkier than rolled oats and have a nuttier flavor, which makes them perfect once baby is ready for some texture. Makes 1½ cups (351 g).

INGREDIENTS

½ cup (40 g) steel cut oats, rinsed

3 cups (710 ml) water, divided

METHOD

1. Put a trivet in the bottom of the pressure cooking pot and add 1 cup (235 ml) water.

2. In a 7-inch (18 cm) cake pan, stir together the oats and 2 cups (475 ml) water. Use a sling to carefully lower the pan onto the trivet. Lock the lid in place. Select High Pressure and 14 minutes cook time.

3. When the cook time ends, turn off the pressure cooker. Let the pressure release naturally for 12 minutes, then finish with a quick pressure release. When the float valve drops, carefully remove the lid.

4. Use the sling to remove the pan from the pressure cooking pot and fluff the oats with a fork. Allow to cool for 20 minutes.

5. Transfer the cooled oats to a bowl. For younger eaters, use a baby food mill to puree until smooth.

TIP

Steel cut oats are a blank slate—they pair well with pretty much any fruit puree or diced fruit, and the hearty oats help your baby stay full.

POLENTA (CORN)

Since polenta is made from ground cornmeal, it is a fantastic first baby food for those concerned about gluten. Making polenta in the pressure cooker is so much easier than making it on the stovetop! Makes 1½ cups (363 g).

INGREDIENTS

½ cup (70 g) coarse polenta

2 cups (475 ml) water, divided

METHOD

1. Put a trivet in the bottom of the pressure cooking pot and add 1 cup (235 ml) water.

2. In a 7-inch (18 cm) cake pan, combine the polenta and 1 cup (235 ml) water and stir to ensure the polenta is completely submerged. Use a sling to carefully lower the pan onto the trivet. Lock the lid in place. Select High Pressure and 5 minutes cook time.

3. When the cook time ends, turn off the pressure cooker. Let the pressure release naturally for 10 minutes, then finish with a quick pressure release. When the float valve drops, carefully remove the lid.

4. Use the sling to remove the pan from the pressure cooking pot and fluff the polenta with a fork. Allow to cool for 20 minutes.

5. Serve as prepared or mix with vegetable, meat, or fruit purees.

TIP

If you prefer a smoother texture, you can swap grits for the polenta since both are made from different varieties of dried corn. Traditionally, polenta is made from yellow corn and has a coarser texture, while grits are generally made from white corn and have a finer texture. However, read the labels carefully and avoid polenta or grits that are "quick-cooking" or "instant."

WHITE RICE

Rice cereal has been a classic first food for generations because it's gentle on baby's tummy and unlikely to cause any food sensitivities. The mild flavor makes it easy to introduce to babies. Makes 1½ cups (237 g).

INGREDIENTS

½ cup (93 g) long-grain white rice, rinsed

1⅔ cups (395 ml) water, divided

METHOD

1. Put a trivet in the bottom of the pressure cooking pot and add 1 cup (235 ml) water.

2. In a 7-inch (18 cm) cake pan, combine the rice and ⅔ cup (160 ml) water and stir to ensure the rice is completely submerged. Use a sling to carefully lower the pan onto the trivet. Lock the lid in place. Select High Pressure and 4 minutes cook time.

3. When the cook time ends, turn off the pressure cooker. Let the pressure release naturally for 7 minutes, then finish with a quick pressure release. When the float valve drops, carefully remove the lid.

4. Use the sling to remove the pan from the pressure cooking pot and fluff the rice with a fork. Allow to cool for 20 minutes.

5. For younger eaters, use a baby food mill to puree until smooth. For older eaters, serve as a finger food or mix with a vegetable, meat, or fruit puree.

TIP

To make the rice cook up less sticky, use a hot water rinse and soak. Place the rice in a fine-mesh strainer and rinse well with hot water until the water runs clear. Place the rice in a bowl of hot water and let sit for 30 minutes. Rinse again through a fine-mesh strainer to remove any remaining starch. Drain the water and continue with the recipes as directed.

BROWN RICE

Brown rice and white rice come from the same grain, but brown rice is much higher in B vitamins and fiber, thanks to the bran outer coating. Brown rice lets your baby experience a new, chewy texture and nutty flavor. Makes 1½ cups (293 g).

INGREDIENTS

½ cup (93 g) long-grain brown rice, rinsed

1¾ cups (410 ml) water, divided

METHOD

1. Put a trivet in the bottom of the pressure cooking pot and add 1 cup (235 ml) water.

2. In a 7-inch (18 cm) cake pan, combine the rice and ¾ cup (175 ml) water and stir to ensure the rice is completely submerged. Use a sling to carefully lower the pan onto the trivet. Lock the lid in place. Select High Pressure and 27 minutes cook time.

3. When the cook time ends, turn off the pressure cooker. Let the pressure release naturally for 10 minutes, then finish with a quick pressure release. When the float valve drops, carefully remove the lid.

4. Use the sling to remove the pan from the pressure cooking pot and fluff the rice with a fork. Allow to cool for 20 minutes.

5. For younger eaters, use a baby food mill to puree until smooth. For older eaters, serve as a finger food or mix with a vegetable, meat, or fruit puree.

TIP

To freeze, divide the rice into individual servings using silicone baby food trays. Once frozen, remove the rice from the trays and store in a zipper-top plastic bag.

FARRO (WHEAT)

Farro is an ancient whole grain, and it's lower in gluten than many other wheat varieties, which makes it an excellent way to introduce wheat to your baby's diet. Makes 1½ cups (237 g).

INGREDIENTS

½ cup (104 g) pearled or semi-pearled farro

2 cups (475 ml) water, divided

METHOD

1. Put a trivet in the bottom of the pressure cooking pot and add 1 cup (235 ml) water.

2. In a 7-inch (18 cm) cake pan, combine the farro and 1 cup (235 ml) water and stir to ensure the farro is completely submerged. Use a sling to carefully lower the pan onto the trivet. Lock the lid in place. Select High Pressure and 20 minutes cook time.

3. When the cook time ends, turn off the pressure cooker. Let the pressure release naturally for 10 minutes, then finish with a quick pressure release. When the float valve drops, carefully remove the lid.

4. Use the sling to remove the pan from the pressure cooking pot and fluff the farro with a fork. Allow to cool for 20 minutes.

5. For younger eaters, use a baby food mill to puree until smooth. For older eaters, serve as a finger food or mix with a vegetable, meat, or fruit puree.

TIP

The cook time for farro varies significantly depending on the type of farro grain used, and sometimes, it can be hard to tell what kind of farro your store sells. When in doubt, check the cook time on your package. The whole-grain farro generally has a cook time around 30 to 40 minutes and needs an overnight soak. Semi-pearled and pearled farro have part or all of the bran removed and have a shorter cook time, around 15 to 25 minutes.

COUSCOUS (WHEAT)

Couscous is made from semolina wheat and is an excellent stand-in for pasta in baby food recipes. These chewy yet firm balls are wonderful to eat on their own and even better when mixed with purees. Makes 1½ cups (236 g).

INGREDIENTS

½ cup (86 g) pearl couscous, rinsed

1⅔ cups (395 ml) water, divided

METHOD

1. Put a trivet in the bottom of the pressure cooking pot and add 1 cup (235 ml) water.

2. In a 7-inch (18 cm) cake pan, combine the couscous and ⅔ cup (160 ml) water and stir to ensure the couscous is completely submerged. Use a sling to carefully lower the pan onto the trivet. Lock the lid in place. Select High Pressure and 8 minutes cook time.

3. When the cook time ends, turn off the pressure cooker. Let the pressure release naturally for 2 minutes, then finish with a quick pressure release. When the float valve drops, carefully remove the lid.

4. Use the sling to remove the pan from the pressure cooking pot and fluff the couscous with a fork. Allow to cool for 20 minutes.

5. For younger eaters, use a baby food mill to puree until smooth. For older eaters, serve as a finger food or mix with a vegetable, meat, or fruit puree.

TIP

Couscous comes in a variety of sizes. We prefer the larger pearl couscous; however, if you've purchased a smaller variety like Moroccan couscous, reduce the cook time to 2 minutes.

QUINOA

Quinoa is a gluten-free seed that's also a nutritional powerhouse! Packing lots of protein and iron, all nine amino acids, and lots of fiber, it's a perfect addition to your baby's diet. Makes 1½ cups (278 g).

INGREDIENTS

½ cup (87 g) quinoa, well rinsed

1½ cups (355 ml) water, divided

METHOD

1. Put a trivet in the bottom of the pressure cooking pot and add 1 cup (235 ml) water.

2. In a 7-inch (18 cm) cake pan, combine the quinoa and ½ cup (120 ml) water and stir to ensure the quinoa is completely submerged. Use a sling to carefully lower the pan onto the trivet. Lock the lid in place. Select High Pressure and 4 minutes cook time.

3. When the cook time ends, turn off the pressure cooker. Let the pressure release naturally for 10 minutes, then finish with a quick pressure release. When the float valve drops, carefully remove the lid.

4. Use the sling to remove the pan from the pressure cooking pot and fluff the quinoa with a fork. Allow to cool for 20 minutes.

5. Serve as prepared or mix with vegetable, meat, or fruit purees.

TIP

Even though most quinoa comes prerinsed, we still prefer to give it a good rinse in a mesh strainer until the water runs clear, just to avoid any bitter taste once cooked.

BLACK BEANS

With their dark color, soft texture, and easy-to-pick-up size, well-cooked black beans make an excellent finger food for babies. Makes 2 cups (370 g).

INGREDIENTS

1 cup (180 g) dried black beans, rinsed

3 cups (700 ml) water

METHOD

1. Add the black beans and 3 cups (700 ml) water to the pressure cooking pot and stir. Lock the lid in place. Select High Pressure and 30 minutes cook time.

2. When the cook time ends, turn off the pressure cooker. Let the pressure release naturally for 20 minutes, then finish with a quick pressure release. When the float valve drops, carefully remove the lid.

3. Remove the black beans from the pressure cooking pot and allow to cool for 20 minutes.

4. To serve, you can mash or use a food mill or blender to puree. (Add water if needed to blend but use the minimum amount necessary.)

TIP

If you're worried about the beans making your baby gassy, use the quick soak method. Place the rinsed black beans in the pressure cooking pot and add enough water to cover the beans by 2 inches (5 cm). Lock the lid in place. Select High Pressure and 1 minute cook time.

When the cook time ends, turn off the pressure cooker. Let the beans soak for 1 hour. Remove the lid. Discard any beans that are floating on top of the water and then strain the beans. Discard the cooking water and rinse out the pressure cooking pot.

Return the soaked beans to the pot with a cup (235 ml) water and cook at High Pressure for 6 to 8 minutes. Continue with the recipe as directed.

CHICKPEAS

Like other legumes, chickpeas are a great source of fiber and protein! If your baby has a sensitive tummy, introduce chickpeas a little at a time in combination with a vegetable or meat puree. Makes 2 cups (328 g).

INGREDIENTS

1 cup (200 g) dried chickpeas, rinsed

3 cups (700 ml) water

METHOD

1. Add the chickpeas and 3 cups (700 ml) water to the pressure cooking pot and stir. Lock the lid in place. Select High Pressure and 40 minutes cook time.

2. When the cook time ends, turn off the pressure cooker. Let the pressure release naturally for 20 minutes and then finish with a quick pressure release. When the float valve drops, carefully remove the lid.

3. Remove the chickpeas from the pressure cooking pot and allow to cool for 20 minutes.

4. To serve, you can mash or use a food mill or blender to puree. (Add water if needed to blend but use the minimum amount necessary.)

TIP
You can double the recipe and reserve a portion of the chickpea puree to make hummus for yourself.

LENTILS

Lentils are a good source of protein, fiber, and iron. Mash them up to make a thickener for your meat and dinner purees. Makes 2 cups (396 g).

INGREDIENTS

1 cup (192 g) dried lentils (We use green lentils).

2 cups (475 ml) water

METHOD

1. Spread the lentils on a shallow dish and check for any debris. Add the lentils to a fine-mesh strainer and rinse well.

2. Add the rinsed lentils and 2 cups (475 ml) water to the pressure cooking pot and stir. Lock the lid in place. Select High Pressure and 15 minutes cook time.

3. When the cook time ends, turn off the pressure cooker. Let the pressure release naturally for 10 minutes, then finish with a quick pressure release. When the float valve drops, carefully remove the lid.

4. Remove the lentils from the pressure cooking pot and allow to cool for 20 minutes.

5. To serve, you can mash or use a food mill or blender to puree. (Add water if needed to blend but use the minimum amount necessary.)

TIP

Lentils come in a variety of colors. If your baby doesn't like the ones you serve, pick a different color and try again. Yellow, red, and orange lentils are generally quicker cooking than green or brown, so you may need to reduce the cook time.

CHAPTER 3

FRUIT AND VEGETABLE BLENDS

Once babies have shown that they can handle simple fruits and vegetables and grains, you can expand into more robust flavor combinations and start adding texture. These combinations are meant to be blended with a little more texture, and they work well when mixed with grains, yogurt, or cottage cheese.

APPLE BANANA CARROT PUREE

We love this fruit-vegetable blend, and we think your baby will as well! Apples and carrots are a classic combination, and the banana lends an extra creaminess to the puree. Makes 2 cups (455 g).

INGREDIENTS

3 large soft apples (such as Jonagold, Fuji, or Golden Delicious), peeled, cored, and quartered

3 carrots, peeled and cut into 2-inch (5 cm) pieces

1 medium fresh banana, peeled

1 cup (235 ml) water

METHOD

1. Place a steamer basket in the bottom of the pressure cooker and add 1 cup (235 ml) water. Place the apple and carrot pieces inside the basket. Lock the lid in place. Select High Pressure and 4 minutes cook time.

2. When the cook time ends, turn off the pressure cooker. Let the pressure release naturally for 5 minutes, then finish with a quick pressure release. When the float valve drops, carefully remove the lid.

3. Remove the apples and carrots from the steamer basket, reserving the cooking water. Allow to cool for 20 minutes.

4. Transfer the cooked apples and carrots to a blender jar or food processer. Add the peeled banana and ¼ cup (60 ml) reserved cooking water. Blend until very smooth. (Add more water if needed to blend but use the minimum amount necessary.)

TIP

The riper the banana, the sweeter the puree will be. If you're worried about the puree being too sweet, add half the banana to the puree and dice the other half for finger food.

BANANA BLUEBERRY PEAR PUREE

This flavor combination is a fruit lover's dream! Our babies gobbled it up, and we've been known to steal a couple cubes of these frozen purees to make our own morning smoothies! Makes 2 cups (455 g).

INGREDIENTS

3 large pears, peeled, cored, and quartered

1 cup (145 g) blueberries

1 medium fresh banana, peeled

1 cup (235 ml) water

METHOD

1. Place a steamer basket in the bottom of the pressure cooker and add 1 cup (235 ml) water. Place the pear quarters and blueberries inside the steamer basket. Lock the lid in place. Select High Pressure and 4 minutes cook time.

2. When the cook time ends, turn off the pressure cooker and use a quick pressure release. When the float valve drops, carefully remove the lid.

3. Remove the pears and blueberries from the steamer basket, reserving the cooking water. Allow to cool for 20 minutes.

4. Transfer the cooked pears and blueberries to a blender jar or food processer. Add the peeled banana and ¼ cup (60 ml) reserved cooking water and blend until very smooth. (Add more cooking water if needed to blend but use the minimum amount necessary.)

TIP

You can use fresh or frozen blueberries in this puree without adjusting the cook time.

BLUEBERRY APPLE SPINACH PUREE

The sweet flavor of the apples and blueberries makes it easy for your baby to enjoy spinach. Makes about 2 cups (455 g).

INGREDIENTS

3 large soft apples (such as Jonagold, Fuji, or Golden Delicious), peeled, cored, and quartered

1 cup (145 g) blueberries

1 cup (30 g) tightly packed fresh spinach

1 cup (235 ml) water

METHOD

1. Place a steamer basket in the bottom of the pressure cooker and add 1 cup (235 ml) water. Place the apple pieces, blueberries, and spinach inside the basket. Lock the lid in place. Select High Pressure and 4 minutes cook time.

2. When the cook time ends, turn off the pressure cooker. Let the pressure release naturally for 5 minutes, then finish with a quick pressure release. When the float valve drops, carefully remove the lid.

3. Remove the apples, blueberries, and spinach from the steamer basket, reserving the cooking water. Allow to cool for 20 minutes.

4. Transfer the cooked apples, blueberries, and spinach to a blender jar or food processer. Add ½ cup (120 ml) reserved cooking water. Blend until very smooth. (Add more water if needed to blend but use the minimum amount necessary.)

TIP

This recipe is pretty flexible! If your baby tolerates the spinach well, try increasing the spinach to 2 cups (60 g). You may also want to add more blueberries to keep the blue color.

MANGO PEAR ZUCCHINI PUREE

This puree is an excellent introduction to mango, and mixing fruits and veggies provides your baby with the sweet taste they prefer and the added vitamins and minerals you know they need. Makes 3 cups (675 g).

INGREDIENTS

2 pears, peeled, cored, and quartered

1 fresh zucchini, sliced into 2-inch (5 cm) pieces

2 cups (350 g) frozen mango chunks

1 cup (235 ml) water

METHOD

1. Place a steamer basket in the bottom of the pressure cooker and add 1 cup (235 ml) water. Place the pears, zucchini, and mango inside the steamer basket. Lock the lid in place. Select High Pressure and 4 minutes cook time.

2. When the cook time ends, turn off the pressure cooker. Let the pressure release naturally for 5 minutes, then use a quick pressure release. When the float valve drops, carefully remove the lid.

3. Remove the pears, zucchini, and mango from the steamer basket, reserving the cooking water. Allow to cool for 20 minutes.

4. Transfer the cooked pears, zucchini, and mango to a blender jar or food processer and blend until very smooth. (Add reserved cooking water if needed to blend but use the minimum amount necessary.)

TIP

If desired, you can use fresh mango in this puree, just add it after cooking the zucchini and pears. If you'd rather avoid mango, substitute frozen peaches.

ORANGE CARROT PEACH PUREE

This beautiful orange puree is a sweet blend that babies will love. It's an excellent way to introduce your baby to citrus—cooking the orange makes it gentler on baby's tummy. Makes 1½ cups (340 g).

INGREDIENTS

1 large orange, peeled and halved

2 carrots, peeled and cut into 2-inch (5 cm) pieces

2 large peaches, peeled, pitted, and sliced

1 cup (235 ml) water

METHOD

1. Place a steamer basket in the bottom of the pressure cooker and add 1 cup (235 ml) water. Place the orange, carrots, and peaches inside the steamer basket. Lock the lid in place. Select High Pressure and 4 minutes cook time.

2. When the cook time ends, turn off the pressure cooker. Let the steam release naturally for 5 minutes, then finish with a quick pressure release. When the float valve drops, carefully remove the lid. Remove the orange, carrots, and peaches from the steamer basket, reserving the cooking water. Allow to cool for 20 minutes.

3. Transfer the cooked orange, carrots, and peaches to a blender jar or food processer and blend until very smooth. (Add reserved cooking water if needed to blend but use the minimum amount necessary.)

TIP

For thick carrots, cut in half lengthwise and then slice into 2-inch (5 cm) pieces.

PEAR AND PINEAPPLE PUREE

This sweet puree is loaded with vitamin C and antioxidants, and it smells so good that you'll want to have a bowlful with your baby. Makes 2 cups (455 g).

INGREDIENTS

3 large pears, peeled, cored, and quartered

½ fresh pineapple, cored and diced

1 cup (235 ml) water

METHOD

1. Place the pear quarters, pineapple pieces, and 1 cup (235 ml) water in the pressure cooking pot. Lock the lid in place. Select High Pressure and 4 minutes cook time.

2. When the cook time ends, turn off the pressure cooker. Let the pressure release naturally for 5 minutes, then use a quick pressure release. When the float valve drops, carefully remove the lid. Remove the pear and pineapple using a slotted spoon, reserving the cooking water. Allow to cool for 20 minutes.

3. Transfer the pear and pineapple to a blender jar or food processer and blend until very smooth. (Add reserved cooking water if needed to blend but use the minimum amount necessary.)

TIP

If you want, you can add the other half of the pineapple to the Mango Pear Zucchini Puree on page 77 for a tropical twist. Or, just dice the remaining half of the pineapple, place it on skewers, and grill it to enjoy yourself.

STRAWBERRY APPLESAUCE

This classic fruit blend is a kid favorite for a reason—it's sweet and delicious! Making it at home allows you to control the sugar content, and the pressure cooker makes it quicker than ever. Makes 3 to 4 cups (675 to 900g).

INGREDIENTS

5 large soft apples (such as Jonagold, Fuji, or Golden Delicious), peeled, cored, and quartered

2 cups (290 g) strawberries, washed and hulled

1 cup (235 ml) water

METHOD

1. Place a steamer basket in the bottom of the pressure cooker and add 1 cup (235 ml) water. Place the apples and strawberries inside the steamer basket. Lock the lid in place. Select High Pressure and 4 minutes cook time.

2. When the cook time ends, turn off the pressure cooker. Let the pressure release naturally for 5 minutes, then use a quick pressure release. When the float valve drops, carefully remove the lid.

3. Remove the apples and strawberries from the steamer basket, reserving the cooking water. Allow to cool for 20 minutes.

4. Place the steamed apples and strawberries in a blender jar or food processer. Add ¼ cup (60 ml) reserved cooking water and blend until very smooth. (Add more water if needed to blend but use the minimum amount necessary.)

TIP

Using red apples will make the puree sweeter, and green apples will make the puree more tart. We generally use two or three different kinds of apples to balance the flavor between sweet and tart.

STRAWBERRY PEACH BANANA PUREE

The strawberries and peaches give this puree a vibrant pink color and the banana adds a smooth texture. Makes 2 cups (455 g).

INGREDIENTS

3 large peaches, peeled, pitted, and sliced

2 cups (290 g) strawberries, hulled

1 medium fresh banana, peeled

1 cup (235 ml) water

METHOD

1. Place a steamer basket in the bottom of the pressure cooker and add 1 cup (235 ml) water. Place the peaches and strawberries inside the steamer basket. Lock the lid in place. Select High Pressure and 4 minutes cook time.

2. When the cook time ends, turn off the pressure cooker. Let the steam release naturally for 10 minutes, then use a quick pressure release. When the float valve drops, carefully remove the lid.

3. Remove the peaches and strawberries from the steamer basket, reserving the cooking water. Allow to cool for 20 minutes.

4. Transfer the cooked peaches and strawberries to a blender jar or food processer and add the banana. Blend until very smooth. (Add reserved cooking water if needed to blend but use the minimum amount necessary.)

TIP

If desired, you can simply cut the peaches in half with the skin on and remove the pit. The skin will easily come off after pressure cooking.

BUTTERNUT SQUASH AND SWEET CORN PUREE

Turn a slightly sweet butternut squash into a beautiful puree. This was always one of our babies' favorites. Makes 1 ½ cups (340 g).

INGREDIENTS

2 cups (280 g) frozen diced butternut squash

1 cup (164 g) frozen sweet corn

1 cup (235 ml) water

METHOD

1. Place a steamer basket in the bottom of the pressure cooker and add 1 cup (235 ml) water. Place the butternut squash and corn inside the steamer basket. Lock the lid in place. Select High Pressure and 4 minutes cook time.

2. When the cook time ends, turn off the pressure cooker and use a quick pressure release. When the float valve drops, carefully remove the lid.

3. Remove the butternut squash and corn from the steamer basket, reserving the cooking water. Allow to cool for 20 minutes.

4. Transfer the cooked butternut squash and corn to a blender jar or food processer. Add ¼ cup (60 ml) reserved cooking water and blend until very smooth. (Add more water if needed to blend but use the minimum amount necessary.)

TIP

If using fresh butternut squash, follow the Butternut Squash Puree recipe (page 50) to cook the squash and steam the corn separately with a 0-minute cook time while the squash cools. See Peach Puree (page 48) for how to set your pressure cooker if it doesn't have a 0-minute cook time.

CARROT AND SWEET POTATO PUREE

This classic flavor combination makes a bright orange puree that's loaded with potassium and vitamins A and C. Makes 3 cups (675 g).

INGREDIENTS

4 fresh carrots, peeled and ends trimmed

1 large sweet potato, peeled and cut into 1-inch (1.3 cm) cubes

1 cup (235 ml) water

METHOD

1. Place a steamer basket in the bottom of the pressure cooker and add 1 cup (235 ml) water. Place the carrots and sweet potato inside the steamer basket. Lock the lid in place. Select High Pressure and 8 minutes cook time.

2. When the cook time ends, turn off the pressure cooker. Let the pressure release naturally for 10 minutes, then finish with a quick pressure release. When the float valve drops, carefully remove the lid.

3. Remove the carrots and sweet potato from the steamer basket, reserving the cooking water. Allow to cool for 20 minutes.

4. Place the steamed carrots and sweet potato in a blender jar or food processer. Add ¾ cup (175 ml) reserved cooking water and blend until very smooth. (Add more water if needed to blend but use the minimum amount necessary.)

TIP

For recipes with longer cook times like this one, you can leave your carrots whole and they'll still cook through.

GREEN BEAN AND SWEET CORN PUREE

If green beans are too bitter for your baby, try sweetening them with corn. This blend is a gorgeous light-green puree that just might change your baby's mind about green beans. Makes 2 cups (455 g).

INGREDIENTS

2 cups (248 g) frozen green beans

1 cup (164 g) frozen sweet corn

1 cup (235 ml) water

METHOD

1. Place a steamer basket in the bottom of the pressure cooker and add 1 cup (235 ml) water. Place the green beans and corn inside the steamer basket. Lock the lid in place. Select High Pressure and 3 minutes cook time.

2. When the cook time ends, turn off the pressure cooker. Use a quick pressure release. When the float valve drops, carefully remove the lid. Remove the green beans and corn from the steamer basket, reserving the cooking water. Allow to cool for 20 minutes.

3. Transfer the cooked green beans and corn to a blender jar or food processer. Add ½ cup (120 ml) reserved cooking water and blend until very smooth. (Add more water if needed to blend but use the minimum amount necessary.)

TIP

We used frozen green beans and frozen corn in this recipe because of the convenience and year-round great taste. However, if you wish to use fresh green beans and corn right off the cob, use 2 cups (200 g) fresh green beans, washed, trimmed, and diced into 2-inch (5 cm) pieces, and 1 ear fresh corn, shucked and broken in half. Cook at High Pressure for 3 minutes and use a quick pressure release.

MASHED POTATOES WITH CAULIFLOWER

Cauliflower is a good source of vitamins and fiber, and it is a great way to get some nutrition into your mashed potatoes. Makes 2 cups (455 g).

INGREDIENTS

2 medium-size russet potatoes, peeled and quartered

½ cup (50 g) chopped cauliflower florets

1 cup (235 ml) water

METHOD

1. Place a steamer basket in the bottom of the pressure cooker and add 1 cup (235 ml) water. Place the potatoes and cauliflower inside the steamer basket. Lock the lid in place. Select High Pressure and 5 minutes cook time.

2. When the cook time ends, turn off the pressure cooker. Use a quick pressure release. When the float valve drops, carefully remove the lid. Use a fork to test the potatoes. If needed, relock the lid and cook at High Pressure for a few minutes more.

3. Remove the potatoes and cauliflower from the steamer basket, reserving the cooking water. Allow to cool for 20 minutes.

4. Use a ricer or baby food mill to mash the potatoes and cauliflower together until mostly smooth. Stir in ¼ cup (60 ml) reserved cooking water, a little at a time, until the potatoes are the desired texture.

TIP

Reserve some of the mashed potatoes and cauliflower puree. Add milk, butter, salt, and pepper to taste and you've made a delicious and healthy side dish for your meal. Make a double or triple batch to feed your whole family.

SWEET CORN, SPAGHETTI SQUASH, AND SPINACH PUREE

This vegetable blend is a baby favorite—the sweetness of the corn and spaghetti squash soften the sharp taste of spinach. Makes 3 cups (675 g).

INGREDIENTS

1 fresh spaghetti squash (about 2 pounds, or 900 g)

1 cup (164 g) frozen corn

1 cup (30 g) tightly packed fresh spinach

2 cups (475 ml) water, divided

METHOD

1. Wash the spaghetti squash. Do not peel. Use a sharp knife to remove the stem end of the squash, cut the squash in half vertically, and remove the seeds with a spoon.

2. Add 1 cup (235 ml) water to the pressure cooking pot. Add a trivet to the pot and carefully place the spaghetti squash pieces on top. Lock the lid in place. Select High Pressure and 8 minutes cook time.

3. When the cook time ends, turn off the pressure cooker. Let the pressure release naturally for 2 minutes, then finish with a quick pressure release. When the float valve drops, carefully remove the lid.

4. Remove the spaghetti squash from the cooking pot, reserving the cooking water. Allow to cool until comfortable to handle and then remove the skin. Divide the spaghetti squash in half. Use one half for this recipe and set aside the other half.

5. Place a steamer basket in the bottom of the pressure cooker and add 1 cup (235 ml) water. Place the corn and spinach inside the steamer basket. Lock the lid in place. Select High Pressure and 0 minutes cook time.

6. When the cook time ends, turn off the pressure cooker. Use a quick pressure release. When the valve drops, carefully remove the lid.

7. Remove the corn and spinach from the steamer basket. Discard the cooking water. Allow to cool for 20 minutes.

8. Place the cooked spaghetti squash, corn, and spinach in a blender jar or food processer. Add ½ cup (120 ml) of the reserved squash cooking water and blend until very smooth. (Add more water if needed to blend but use the minimum amount necessary.)

TIP

This recipe is easily doubled with no change to the cook time if you'd like to use the entire spaghetti squash. Or, substitute the other half of the spaghetti squash for the frozen butternut squash in the Butternut Squash and Sweet Corn Puree (page 82).

SWEET PEA AND AVOCADO PUREE

Avocados are a fantastic food for babies; they're high in potassium and fiber, and they give this pea puree a smooth and creamy texture. Makes 2 cups (455 g).

INGREDIENTS

2 cups shelled peas; (300 g) fresh or (260 g) frozen

1 large avocado, halved, pitted, and peeled

1 cup (235 ml) water

METHOD

1. Place a steamer basket in the bottom of the pressure cooker and add 1 cup (235 ml) water. Place the peas inside the steamer basket. Lock the lid in place. Select High Pressure and 2 minutes cook time.

2. When the cook time ends, turn off the pressure cooker. Use a quick pressure release. When the float valve drops, carefully remove the lid. Remove the peas from the steamer basket, reserving the cooking water. Allow to cool for 20 minutes.

3. Transfer the cooked peas to a blender jar or food processer. Add the avocado and 1 cup (235 ml) reserved cooking water. Blend until very smooth. (Add more water if needed to blend but use the minimum amount necessary.)

TIP

Avocados are loaded with healthy fats and are a wonderful addition to baby's diet. Our testers didn't have any problem with them browning in this recipe; however, if you're worried, you can add a little mashed avocado to individual servings of pea puree.

SWEET PEA, ZUCCHINI, AND GREEN BEAN PUREE

Get your greens! The sweet peas and mild zucchini balance the green bean flavor in this all-vegetable blend. Makes 2 cups (455 g).

INGREDIENTS

2 cups shelled peas, (300g) fresh or (260 g) frozen

1 fresh zucchini, sliced into 2-inch (5 cm) pieces

1 cup (124 g) frozen green beans

1 cup (235 ml) water

METHOD

1. Place a steamer basket in the bottom of the pressure cooker and add 1 cup (235 ml) water. Place the peas, zucchini, and green beans inside the basket. Lock the lid in place. Select High Pressure and 3 minutes cook time.

2. When the cook time ends, turn off the pressure cooker. Use a quick pressure release. When the float valve drops, carefully remove the lid.

3. Remove the vegetables from the steamer basket, reserving the cooking water. Allow to cool for 20 minutes.

4. Place the steamed vegetables in a blender jar or food processer. Add ¼ cup (60 ml) reserved cooking water and blend until very smooth. (Add more water if needed to blend but use the minimum amount necessary.)

TIP
If substituting fresh green beans, add 2 minutes to the cook time.

CHAPTER 4

MEATS AND DINNERS

Our babies didn't enjoy the store-bought baby food meats; however, they loved when we started serving them homemade dishes that included meat. This section begins with single-ingredient meats and then expands to include simple meat and veggie dinners. If your baby is hesitant to accept meats at first, try serving them with a favorite vegetable puree.

CHICKEN PUREE

Chicken is high in protein and B vitamins, and it makes an ideal first meat for baby. This simple chicken puree calls for chicken thighs, which have a higher fat content and cook up moist and tender in the pressure cooker. Makes 2 cups (455 g).

INGREDIENTS

1 pound (455 g) boneless skinless chicken thighs, trimmed and diced

1 fresh carrot, peeled and cut into 2-inch (5 cm) pieces, optional, for color

1 cup (235 ml) water

METHOD

1. Add the chicken, carrot (if using), and 1 cup (235 ml) water to the pressure cooking pot. Lock the lid in place. Select High Pressure and 4 minutes cook time.

2. When the cook time ends, turn off the pressure cooker. Use a quick pressure release. When the float valve drops, carefully remove the lid.

3. Use an instant-read thermometer to check the chicken for doneness (see page 36). Remove the chicken and carrot from the cooking pot, reserving the cooking water. (You can skim off the fat if you prefer.) Allow to cool until comfortable to handle.

4. Place the chicken in a blender jar or food processer. Pulse the blender to grind the meat, adding a little reserved cooking water if necessary to blend. If you're using a high-powered blender to blend the chicken completely smooth, you'll need less water than if you want it to remain textured. Add ½ to ¾ cup (120 to 175 ml) reserved cooking water and blend until the desired consistency is reached. (Add more water if needed to blend but use the minimum amount necessary.)

TIP

If you prefer, you can use diced chicken breasts without changing the cook time.

TURKEY PUREE

Turkey contains more protein, B vitamins, and iron than chicken and is lower in cholesterol. It's another great first meat for baby. Makes 2 cups (455 g).

INGREDIENTS

1 pound (455 g) fresh ground turkey

1 fresh carrot, peeled and cut into 2-inch (5 cm) pieces, optional, for color

1 cup (235 ml) water

METHOD

1. Add 1 cup (235 ml) water to the pressure cooking pot. Add a trivet to the pot and carefully place the ground turkey on top (no need to break up the ground turkey), followed by the carrot (if using). Lock the lid in place. Select High Pressure and 6 minutes cook time.

2. When the cook time ends, turn off the pressure cooker. Let the pressure release naturally for 2 minutes, then finish with a quick pressure release. When the float valve drops, carefully remove the lid.

3. Use an instant-read thermometer to check the cooked ground turkey for doneness (see page 36). Remove the ground turkey from the cooking pot, reserving the cooking water. (You can skim off the fat if you prefer.) Allow to cool until comfortable to handle.

4. Place the ground turkey in a blender jar or food processer. Pulse the blender to grind the meat, adding a little reserved cooking water if necessary to blend. If you're using a high-powered blender to blend the turkey completely smooth, you'll need less water than if you want it to remain textured. Add ½ to 1 cup (120 to 235 ml) reserved cooking water and blend until the desired consistency is reached. (Add more water if needed to blend but use the minimum amount necessary.)

TIP

Check your ground turkey to be sure no additional ingredients or spices have been added. This cook time is for fresh, not frozen, turkey that is in a flat block from the grocery store. If your ground turkey is in a round tube shape, you will need more time at high pressure. You can also use this method and cook time to cook ground chicken or ground beef for your baby.

If you prefer, you can also use 1 pound (455 g) of diced turkey in this recipe. Just place the diced turkey directly in the 1 cup (235 ml) water on the bottom of the pressure cooking pot and cook as directed.

PORK PUREE

While cured meats like ham are best avoided with babies, lean cuts of pork are high in protein and B vitamins and low in fat. This simple puree is an excellent way to introduce your baby to pork. Makes 1 ½ to 2 cups (340 to 455 g).

INGREDIENTS

1 pound (455 g) boneless center-cut pork chops, diced

1 to 2 tablespoons (16 g to 32 g) tomato paste, optional, for color

1 cup (235 ml) water

METHOD

1. Add the pork, tomato paste (if using), and 1 cup (235 ml) water to the pressure cooking pot. Lock the lid in place. Select High Pressure and 15 minutes cook time.

2. When the cook time ends, turn off the pressure cooker. Let the pressure release naturally for 10 minutes and then use a quick pressure release. When the float valve drops, carefully remove the lid.

3. Use an instant-read thermometer to check the pork for doneness (see page 36). Remove the cooked pork from the cooking pot, reserving the cooking water. Allow to cool until comfortable to handle.

4. Place the cooked pork in a blender jar or food processer. Pulse the blender to grind the meat, adding a little reserved cooking water if necessary to blend. If you're using a high-powered blender to blend the pork completely smooth, you'll need less water than if you want it to remain textured. Add ½ to ¾ cup (120 to 175 ml) reserved cooking water and blend until the desired consistency is reached. (Add more water if needed to blend but use the minimum amount necessary.)

TIP

For older babies, make a chunky puree and serve over the Mashed Potatoes with Cauliflower on page 85.

BEEF PUREE

Beef is a good source of iron, which is particularly important for breastfed babies. Makes 1½ to 2 cups (340 to 455 g).

INGREDIENTS

1 pound (455 g) beef stew meat, diced (We used cross-rib roast.)

1 to 2 tablespoons (16 g to 32 g) tomato paste, optional, for color

1 cup (235 ml) water

METHOD

1. Add the beef, tomato paste (if using) and 1 cup (235 ml) water to the pressure cooking pot. Lock the lid in place. Select High Pressure and 18 minutes cook time.

2. When the cook time ends, turn off the pressure cooker. Let the pressure release naturally for 5 minutes and then use a quick pressure release. When the float valve drops, carefully remove the lid.

3. Use an instant-read thermometer to check the beef for doneness (see page 36). Remove the cooked beef from the cooking pot, reserving the cooking water. Allow to cool until comfortable to handle.

4. Place the cooked beef in a blender jar or food processer. Pulse the blender to grind the meat, adding a little reserved cooking water if necessary to blend. If you're using a high-powered blender to blend the beef completely smooth, you'll need less water than if you want it to remain textured. Add ¼ to ½ cup (60 to 120 ml) reserved cooking water and blend until the desired consistency is reached. (Add more water if needed to blend but use the minimum amount necessary.)

TIP

If you're serving this as a first food and your baby hasn't yet been introduced to tomatoes, omit the tomato paste. However, the tomato paste adds a great color to the meat and makes it look much more appetizing for baby. Be sure to read the ingredients list and select a tomato paste that doesn't include salt or extra seasonings.

BEEF STEW WITH CARROT, CELERY, AND POTATO

For older babies, this beef stew tastes even better if you brown the beef in a little olive oil before you cook it at high pressure. Makes 2 cups (455 g).

INGREDIENTS

1 pound (455 g) beef stew meat, diced (We used cross-rib roast.)

1 tablespoon (16 g) tomato paste, (optional) for color

1 cup (235 ml) water or low-sodium beef broth

3 fresh carrots, peeled and finely diced

1 rib celery, finely diced

1 small russet potato, peeled and finely diced

METHOD

1. Add the diced beef, tomato paste (if using), and 1 cup (235 ml) water to the pressure cooking pot. Lock the lid in place. Select High Pressure and 17 minutes cook time.

2. When the cook time ends, turn off the pressure cooker and use a quick pressure release. When the float valve drops, carefully remove the lid. Add the vegetables to a steamer basket and place it in the pressure cooker above the beef. Lock the lid in place and select High Pressure and 1 minute cook time.

3. When the cook time ends, turn off the pressure cooker. Allow the pressure to release naturally for 5 minutes and then use a quick pressure release. Remove the steamer basket and vegetables from the cooking pot. Set aside.

4. Use an instant-read thermometer to check the beef for doneness (see page 36). Use a slotted spoon to remove the beef from the pressure cooker, reserving the cooking water. Allow to cool until comfortable to handle.

5. Place about three-quarters of the beef in a blender jar or food processer. Add the reserved cooking water and blend until the desired consistency is reached. (Add more water if needed to blend but use the minimum amount necessary.) Add the remaining portion of beef and pulse to dice the beef without pureeing it.

6. Mix in the steamed vegetables with a spoon. If desired, pulse the vegetables in the blender or food processor to the desired consistency.

TIP
Dice the carrots, celery, and potatoes into smaller pieces to avoid choking hazards. Before serving, make sure the beef you serve your baby is well diced and each bite is separated into individual pieces.

CHICKEN AND RICE

This mix of chicken and rice can be as smooth or as textured as you like. Add diced vegetables and it's a complete meal! Makes 1½ to 2 cups (340 to 455 g).

INGREDIENTS

1 pound (455 g) (about 4) boneless skinless chicken thighs, trimmed, diced

1 fresh carrot, peeled and cut into 2-inch (5 cm) pieces

1 cup (235 ml) water or low-sodium chicken broth

½ cup (98 g) white rice

⅔ cup (60 ml) water

½ cup (91 g) frozen diced vegetable mix, steamed, optional

METHOD

1. Add the diced chicken, carrot, and 1 cup (235 ml) water to the pressure cooking pot. Place a trivet above the items in the cooking pot.

2. In a 7-inch (18 cm) cake pan, stir together the rice and ⅔ cup (160 ml) water. Use a sling to carefully lower the pan onto the trivet. Lock the lid in place. Select High Pressure and 4 minutes cook time.

3. When the cook time ends, turn off the pressure cooker. Let the pressure release naturally for 7 minutes and then finish with a quick pressure release. When the float valve drops, carefully remove the lid. Use the sling to remove the pan from the pressure cooking pot. Stir the rice well and allow to cool.

4. Use an instant-read thermometer to check the chicken for doneness (see page 36). Remove the diced chicken and carrot from the cooking pot, reserving the cooking water. Allow to cool until comfortable to handle.

5. Place the diced chicken and carrot in a blender jar or food processor. Add ¾ cup (175 ml) reserved cooking water and blend until the desired consistency is reached. (Add more water if needed to blend but use the minimum amount necessary.)

6. If using, pulse the steamed vegetables in the blender or food processor to the desired consistency. Add as much rice as desired and mix with a spoon.

TIP

Reserve some of the chicken for older eaters. Add it to the blender jar after pureeing and pulse two or three times to shred. Remove from the blender jar and add steamed rice and vegetables, if desired.

CHICKEN AND PASTA IN BUTTERNUT SQUASH PUREE

The thick butternut squash puree makes this a wholesome meal for babies learning to use a spoon. Makes 2 cups (455 g).

INGREDIENTS

½ pound (225 g) boneless skinless chicken thighs, diced into baby-sized pieces (less than ½ inch [1.3 cm] in all directions)

¼ cup (42 g) orzo pasta

1 cup (235 ml) water or low-sodium chicken broth

3 cups (420 g) frozen diced butternut squash

METHOD

1. Add the diced chicken, orzo, and 1 cup (235 ml) water to the pressure cooking pot. Place a steamer basket inside the cooking pot and place the butternut squash on top. Lock the lid in place. Select High Pressure and 4 minutes cook time.

2. When the cook time ends, turn off the pressure cooker. Let the pressure release naturally for 5 minutes, then finish with a quick pressure release. When the float valve drops, carefully remove the lid. Remove the steamer basket and butternut squash from the cooking pot. Set aside.

3. Use an instant-read thermometer to check the chicken for doneness (see page 36). Use a slotted spoon to remove the chicken and orzo from the pressure cooker, reserving the cooking water. Allow to cool until comfortable to handle.

4. Place the butternut squash in a blender jar or food processer. Add ¼ cup (60 ml) reserved cooking water and blend until the desired consistency is reached. (Add more water if needed to blend but use the minimum amount necessary.) Remove to a bowl and mix in the chicken and orzo with a spoon.

TIP

Orzo pastas can have a broad range of cook times. This recipe was written for orzo with a stovetop cook time between 8 and 11 minutes. If you don't have orzo pasta on hand, you can substitute couscous with no change to the cook time.

TURKEY AND VEGETABLE MEDLEY

This classic combination features lean turkey and nutritious vegetables in a blend your baby will love. Makes 2 cups (455 g).

INGREDIENTS

1 pound (455 g) turkey breast, diced

1 fresh carrot, peeled and cut into 2-inch (5 cm) pieces

1½ cups (355 ml) water or reduced-sodium chicken broth or turkey stock

½ cup (91 g) frozen diced vegetable mix, steamed

METHOD

1. Add the diced turkey, carrot, and 1½ cups (355 ml) water to the pressure cooking pot. Lock the lid in place. Select High Pressure and 6 minutes cook time.

2. When the cook time ends, turn off the pressure cooker. Let the pressure release naturally for 2 minutes, then finish with a quick pressure release. When the float valve drops, carefully remove the lid.

3. Use an instant-read thermometer to check the turkey for doneness (see page 36). Remove the cooked turkey and carrot from the cooking pot, reserving the cooking water. Allow to cool until comfortable to handle.

4. For older eaters, reserve and shred some of the cooked turkey. Place the cooked turkey and carrot in a blender jar or food processer. Add 1½ cups (355 ml) reserved cooking water and blend until the desired consistency is reached. (Add more water if needed to blend but use the minimum amount necessary.)

5. Add the steamed vegetables and mix with a spoon. If desired, pulse the vegetables in the blender or food processor to the desired consistency.

TIP

Steam your frozen vegetables in the pressure cooker while the turkey cools. Place a steamer basket and 1 cup (235 ml) water in the pressure cooker pot. Add the frozen vegetables and select a 0-minute cook time. See Peach Puree (page 48) for how to set your pressure cooker if it doesn't have a 0-minute cook time. Finish with a quick pressure release.

BUTTERNUT SQUASH DINNER

Butternut squash and carrots blend together in a slightly sweet, orange base, and the couscous adds a fun texture for babies who are ready to move beyond purees. Makes 2 cups (455 g).

INGREDIENTS

2 cups (280 g) frozen diced butternut squash

2 fresh carrots, peeled and cut into 2-inch (5 cm) pieces

1¾ cups (410 ml) water, divided

½ cup (86 g) pearl couscous

METHOD

1. Add the squash, carrots, and 1 cup (235 ml) water to the bottom of the pressure cooking pot. Place a trivet above the items in the cooking pot.

2. In a 7-inch (18 cm) cake pan, stir together the couscous and remaining ¾ cup (175 ml) water. Use a sling to carefully lower the pan onto the trivet. Lock the lid in place. Select High Pressure and 5 minutes cook time.

3. When the cook time ends, turn off the pressure cooker. Allow the pressure to release naturally for 2 minutes, then finish with a quick pressure release. When the float valve drops, carefully remove the lid. Use the sling to remove the pan from the pressure cooking pot. Stir the couscous well and allow to cool.

4. Place a fine-mesh strainer above a bowl to separate the squash and carrots from the cooking water, reserving the cooking water. Place the squash and carrots in a blender with ¼ cup (60 ml) reserved cooking water. Blend until smooth. Stir in as much couscous as desired.

TIP

Add tomatoes or corn to this recipe before pressure cooking for even more vegetable goodness.

FRESH GARDEN VEGETABLE AND PASTA MEDLEY

This pasta and vegetable meal is not in a puree to allow your baby to enjoy different colors and textures. Be sure to dice your vegetables finely—less than ½ inch (1.3 cm) in all directions—to make sure it's safe for baby. Makes 2 cups (455 g).

INGREDIENTS

½ cup (84 g) orzo pasta

1 cup (235 ml) water

1 cup (130 g) peeled, diced carrots

1 cup (120 g) diced zucchini

1 cup (120 g) diced yellow squash

METHOD

1. Add the orzo and 1 cup (235 ml) water to the pressure cooking pot. Place a steamer basket on top and add the carrots, zucchini, and yellow squash to the steamer. Lock the lid in place. Select High Pressure and 3 minutes cook time.

2. When the cook time ends, turn off the pressure cooker. Let the pressure release naturally for 3 minutes, then finish with a quick pressure release. When the float valve drops, carefully remove the lid. Remove the steamer basket and vegetables from the cooking pot. Set aside. Use a slotted spoon to remove the orzo from the pressure cooker. Allow to cool until comfortable to handle.

3. Mix the orzo pasta with the vegetables.

   TIP
   You can substitute your baby's favorite vegetables, just make sure they are cut into baby-size pieces.

CHAPTER 5

DESSERTS FOR A FIRST BIRTHDAY CELEBRATION

Jennifer's babies didn't get foods with added sugar until their first birthday, and even then, she liked to keep the sugar content low. Barbara fed her babies healthy foods but allowed for the occasional indulgence. Therefore, we combined our styles and created two fantastic options to celebrate this happy milestone—one healthier, no-sugar-added option and one finger-licking introduction to chocolate for these fun smash cakes.

HEALTHY CARROT SMASH CAKE WITH CREAM CHEESE FROSTING

The first birthday is such a happy milestone. Celebrate the big day with this no-sugar-added carrot cake that's lightly sweetened with just maple syrup. Makes one 4-inch (10 cm) smash cake.

INGREDIENTS

Nonstick baking spray with flour

⅓ cup (42 g) all-purpose flour

½ teaspoon baking powder

¾ teaspoon pumpkin pie spice

⅛ teaspoon salt

3 tablespoons (45 ml) maple syrup

2 tablespoons (28 ml) olive oil

2 tablespoons (28 ml) milk

1 egg yolk

½ teaspoon vanilla extract

¼ cup (28 g) finely grated carrot

¼ cup (35 g) raisins

1 cup (235 ml) water

Cream Cheese Frosting

2 tablespoons (30 ml) cream cheese, softened

2 tablespoons (30 ml) plain Greek yogurt

1 tablespoon (15 ml) pure maple syrup

METHOD

1. Coat a 4-inch (10 cm) cake pan with nonstick baking spray with flour.

2. In a small bowl, add the flour, baking powder, pumpkin pie spice, and salt and whisk until combined. Set aside.

3. In a large mixing bowl, whisk the maple syrup, olive oil, milk, egg yolk, and vanilla together until well blended. Add the dry ingredients and mix until just blended. Fold in the carrots and raisins. Spoon the batter into the prepared pan.

4. Pour 1 cup (235 ml) water into the pressure cooker cooking pot and place a trivet in the bottom. Carefully center the filled pan on a sling and lower the pan onto the trivet. Lock the lid in place. Select High Pressure and 16 minutes cook time.

5. When the cook time ends, turn off the pressure cooker. Let the pressure release naturally for 10 minutes, then finish with a quick pressure release. When the float valve drops, carefully remove the lid.

6. With the sling, transfer the pan to a wire rack to cool, uncovered, for 5 minutes. Gently loosen the edges, remove the cake from the pan, transfer to a wire rack, and cool completely.

7. *Prepare the Cream Cheese Frosting*: In a large bowl, combine the cream cheese, yogurt, and maple syrup. Using a handheld electric mixer, mix the ingredients on medium speed until smooth. Spread on top of the cooled cake and decorate as desired.

TIP

To make your own pumpkin pie spice, mix ½ teaspoon ground cinnamon, ¼ teaspoon ground ginger, ¼ teaspoon ground nutmeg, and ⅛ teaspoon ground cloves for 1 teaspoon pumpkin pie spice.

CHOCOLATE-CHOCOLATE SMASH CAKE

There's nothing quite like baby's first taste of chocolate cake! This cute little smash cake is topped with a rich, easy-to-make chocolate ganache that your one-year-old will be licking off their sweet little fingers. Makes one 4-inch (10 cm) smash cake.

INGREDIENTS

Nonstick baking spray with flour

3 tablespoons (45 ml) milk

2 tablespoons (28 ml) olive oil

1 large egg yolk

1 teaspoon vanilla extract

¼ cup (50 g) sugar

¼ cup (31 g) all-purpose flour

2 tablespoons (10 g) cocoa powder

½ teaspoon baking powder

⅛ teaspoon salt

1 cup (235 ml) water

Chocolate Ganache

1 tablespoon (15 ml) heavy cream

1½ ounces (42 g) milk chocolate, finely chopped

Sprinkles or chocolate curls for decorating

METHOD

1. Coat a 4-inch (10 cm) cake pan with nonstick baking spray with flour.

2. In a large bowl, whisk the milk, olive oil, egg yolk, and vanilla until blended. Whisk in the sugar. Put a fine-mesh strainer over the top of the bowl and add the flour, cocoa powder, baking powder, and salt. Shake to sift the ingredients into the mixing bowl with the wet ingredients and whisk just until blended. Pour into the prepared pan.

3. Pour 1 cup (235 ml) water into the pressure cooker cooking pot and place a trivet in the bottom. Carefully center the filled pan on a sling and lower the pan onto the trivet. Lock the lid in place. Select High Pressure and 13 minutes cook time.

4. When the cook time ends, turn off the pressure cooker. Let the pressure release naturally for 10 minutes and then finish with a quick pressure release. When the float valve drops, carefully remove the lid. Transfer the pan to a wire rack to cool for 5 minutes. Run a knife around the edge to loosen the cake, then invert onto the rack to cool completely.

5. *Prepare the chocolate ganache:* In a small microwave-safe dish, heat the cream in the microwave just until it starts to bubble around the edges. Add the chopped chocolate and stir until smooth. (If necessary, heat in the microwave on medium power to melt the chocolate.) Allow the ganache to cool on the counter until it is thick and spreadable. Spoon the ganache on top of the cooled cake. Decorate with sprinkles or chocolate curls as desired.

TIP

Using olive oil cuts saturated fat in your baking and adds antioxidants and vitamin E to your baked goods. The olive oil in this recipe doesn't add a strong flavor, but it has natural emulsifiers that help keep the cake moist and delicious. If you prefer, you can substitute vegetable oil.

Acknowledgments

First, I want to thank all my Pressure Cooking Today readers and members of the various Facebook communities, who share their enthusiasm for pressure cooking with me. They keep me energized and striving to create new and innovative recipes and to find new ways to use the electric pressure cooker.

Thank you to my publisher for seeing the need for making baby food quickly and easily in an electric pressure cooker.

Thanks to my husband, who is my indispensable slicer and dicer in the kitchen. He makes recipe creation so much easier, and he makes it more fun to cook.

Finally, thanks to my amazing, talented daughter who put her heart and soul into this cookbook. She spent hours researching dietary recommendations for babies so that the recipes are based on the most up-to-date information available. Her attention to detail is unmatched, and she made sure that every recipe in the cookbook is one that she will be happily using to feed her new little baby joining the family in October 2018.

—*Barbara*

This book wouldn't be possible without my family, and I am deeply grateful for them.

First and foremost, to my mother, for your unfailing belief that someone as distracted as me could ever be a good cook. Thank you for inviting me to help in your kitchen and with your websites. I am so grateful for the opportunities you've provided me and am thrilled to join you on this pressure cooking journey.

To my father, for being happy to help however needed, from lending a hand in the kitchen to watching my boys so I could write.

To my boys, for happily suggesting recipe ideas, taste-testing recipes, and providing candid feedback. Thank you for eating toddler meals for breakfast, lunch, and dinner and having baby foods for snacks and dessert. I love watching you grow and can't wait to see what you do next.

And finally, to my husband, whose contributions to this cookbook are innumerable and whose steady support made it possible. You are truly my partner on this journey, and I just adore you.

—*Jennifer*

About the Authors

Barbara Schieving is a veteran mom of four grown children. She is widely admired cook, writer, and photographer whose two blogs, *Pressure Cooking Today* and *Barbara Bakes*, delight over half a million readers each month with her fabulous, family-friendly recipes and conversational style. Her most recent cookbook, *Instantly Sweet* (2018), written with Marci Buttars, introduces readers to the sweet side of electric pressure cooking, with 75 delicious desserts and sweet treats. Her other cookbooks include *The Electric Pressure Cooker Cookbook* (2017), which features 200 delicious recipes made pressure-cooker fast with fresh and familiar ingredients, and *Simply Sweet Dream Puffs* (2015), which features a wide variety of easy-to-make cream puffs, eclairs, and profiteroles. She lives in the Salt Lake City, Utah, area.

Jennifer Schieving McDaniel is a busy mother of three. She fell in love with pressure cooking when she and her husband lived with her parents while building a new home and is now a huge pressure cooker enthusiast. She uses her pressure cooker every day, often several times a day, to prepare nutritious family meals and can't wait to make these recipes for the little one who recently joined their family. Jennifer and her husband love sharing their pressure cooking expertise and often teach friends, family, and groups how easy it is to cook great meals in the pressure cooker. Jennifer is the managing editor for *Pressure Cooking Today* and is an integral part of the *Pressure Cooking Today* team. She creates recipes, writes how-to posts, answers readers' questions, and so much more. She lives near Barbara in the Salt Lake City, Utah, area.

INDEX